MW01240637

How to Make Your
Relationship
Worth Its Weight
In Gold

By

Israel A. Abejoye

Contents

Acknowledgment

I thank God Almighty for the success of this book. To him, I give my unending gratitude for wisdom, knowledge and understanding as they were essential to put these words together. I also thank my family, friends and loved ones for their supports.

Dedication

I dedicate this book to the real lovers, single parents, widows, orphans, needy, less privileges, those in despair and those striving so hard to make it through. I want to assure you that very soon your dreams shall come true and that very special person that your heart really desires shall be yours.

Prologue

Relationships are very important to the existence of all mankind as our day-to-day activities require that we connect with another person. This is why no man is an island — no one can survive alone — and this makes all man social animals. Relationship is defined as the way in which two or more people or things are connected, so in other words, relationship is the connection or link that exists between or amongst two or more persons. Relationship is synonymous to connection, link, association, affiliation, correspondence, correlation, alliance and etcetera. Relationship can be basically categorised into: family, spiritual, acquaintanceship, friendship, romantic, sexual and marital relationships. Hence, our relationships with other people, our surroundings, the entire universe and The Almighty are very important as they determine our successes in life. Since our relationships with others determine our achievements in life, it is imperative that we learn about relationships so as to understand how they work and how to manage them. This book shall examine the various types of love and their relationships, and help you to distinctively identify one from the other. More often than not, love is what brings about the connection between or amongst two or more persons, or The Almighty and obviously this does not have to be romantic or marital relationship. My point is that there are various types of love with their unique natures, and it is important that you learn each of them so as not to mistake one for another. Additionally, I shall be exploring the natures of love, qualities, characteristics, benefits, do's and don'ts, in order to help you distinguish one from another and apply the right one in the right situation and for its right purpose.

On this account, helping you to work out your relationship becomes my obligation and this is the main reason that I have decided to write this book. Although this book shall examine other types of love but it shall focus more on romantic and marital relationships thus, wherever you find 'relationship' in this book, it most likely implies 'romantic or marital relationship' except if clearly stated. This makes it imperative for you to read every portion of this book without skipping one let alone a page in order to achieve its absolute aims and benefits. To begin with, let us learn what love is, and the various definitions given to love.

What is Love?

Dictionary meanings include, 'strong attraction and desire towards another', 'strong affection and tenderness felt by lovers', in addition to these definitions, love has also been interpreted as words like, commitment, care, passion, trust, submissiveness, tolerance, patience, forgiveness, humility, respect and other virtues that love possess. All these qualities are very important ingredients in every relationship as they are the characteristics of love, so when a relationship lacks any of them, such relationship may not be as effective as it ought to be, in that case, either of the partners or spouses who lacks any of them needs to adjust for the sake of ensuring that it does not become a real big issue in their relationship. Similarly, in this book, it is ideal that I examine the various types of love according to the Greek and their characteristics with regard to helping you understand your romantic or marital relationship better and also finding apt solutions to issues when they come up.

According to <u>Sarah Regan</u>[1] in her article titled, The 8 Types Of Love + How To Know Which One You're Feeling,

---

[1] R. Sarah, (2021). "The 8 Types Of Love + How To Know Which One You're Feeling" {Online}. Available: <u>http://www.mindbodygreen.com/articles/types-of-love</u> {2021-9-21}.

there are Eight (8) types of Love, these are: Eros; which is all about romance, passion, and attraction, Pragma; which develops into practical love, referencing the type of love grounded in duty, commitment, and practicality, Ludus; is very flirtatious and fun, without the strings that come with Eros or Pragma, Agape; which is selfless love, like the type one may associate with saintly figures like Mother Teresa or activists like Malala Yousafzai, Philia; which is a platonic love that develops over a deep, long-lasting friendship, Philautia; which is the love that is all about self-love and self-compassion, Storge; which is the love shared between family members (typically immediate family), and sometimes close family friends or friends from childhood and lastly, Mania; which connotes obsessive love.

In my explanations and instances, I shall be referring to any of these types of love so as to help you understand which one your relationship is based on, and perhaps may be one of the reasons that your relationship is what it is at the moment. Having said this, this book is not to explore love in its widest sense, because love cannot be quantified neither can it be measured, but I will only expound love as wide as I can because love can only be experienced — it is practical — and various persons will tell something different about love based on how it occurs to them. Some persons have found true love while some have never experienced it. Those that have found it can tell that true love really exists but those that never did would tell something really different about it, so believe me when I say that love is what you see it to be however, your perception about love does not change the true nature of love. Therefore, we may want to ask why romantic and marital relationships work out for some persons but never worked out for others — could it be as a result of them falling in love without having the slightest idea of the type of love they feel for their partners or spouses?

Or could it be as a result of their inability to discern if their partners or spouses also possess the right quantity or characteristics of love that they claim they feel for them? This shall be examined in the Chapter One of this book as I discuss the Nature of Love. Love is a mystery! Why do I say this? Even some of those that believe that they know so much about love still finds it really hard to make their relationships thrive, I mean, their love lives are not stable. So, would you rather remain naive of love or become an experienced lover? More of this shall be discussed in the Chapter Seven of this book. True love is hard to find, and yeah, I must admit that it is indeed hard to find but I can assure you that it is worth the risks and sacrifices in the end. There are certain qualities that a true lover must look out for when finding true love and this shall be discussed in the Chapters Two and Ten of this book.

This book is written with the intention to assist every lover which includes young adults, singles, fresh couples and other married couples that still have not gotten it right in their marriages, to make their relationships successful. It is a complete guide for those who intend to go into a romantic or marital relationship — fresh couples or other married ones who are still willing to adjust so as to make their marriages flourish. Each chapter is unique as they individually and collectively shed light on the title of the book which still boils down to helping them achieve long-lasting relationships and of course, successful marriages.

It occurs to me that many young lads and lasses out there have been deluded as a result of the misuse of the word 'love', and perhaps, due to how some of them have been maltreated in their previous relationships or their knowledge from the negative relationship experiences of others, they have come up with phrases like: 'Love is a scam', 'it is only a fool that falls in love', 'true love only exist in books and movies', 'marriage is overrated' and others. Some of them already made up their minds never to love anyone genuinely anymore, since the experiences in their previous relationships have probably made them cynical about every other person that comes their ways. The truth about true love is that it really do exist but lovers, especially young lovers, need to know how to find true lovers and identity them when they come across them. Sometimes, young lovers also need to know about the irony of love: "Those we truly love do not really love us while those we do not love are the ones that love us most," which is one of the reasons that you may want to agree that love can be found in a hopeless place. Another reason that this book is written is to alleviate the prevalence of broken homes, single parents and domestic violence that have taken over our communities in this modern time. Can we conclude that civilisation comes with all this or perhaps love is losing its strong bond? Or could it be as a result of lovers not knowing the qualities, nature, types or characteristics of the love that they feel about their partners or spouse? All these shall be discussed in this book and a good number of advices, opinions and experiences are also shared by great philosophers, scholars and love experts through the author.

Chapter One

The Nature of Love

The nature of love is the innate characteristics of love — the framework or setup in which love exists on or uses to carry out its acts. Love in its true form is natural to all humans. Having defined the nature of love, Cate briefly states that:

> *"I believe there are some things in life you can't deny or rationalize, and [love] is one of them."*
> Cate Blanchett[2]

This makes love a necessity for every man but in order for you to get your relationship right, you must know the true nature of what you feel for your partner or spouse. The objective of this chapter is like asking why does one fall in love with another, that is, what is the basis of one's love for another? The nature of what a couple feels for each other is what determines the kind of actions or doings that are expected of them in their relationship. For instance, the nature of love that a mother feels for her children is quite different from what she feels for herself, husband, friends,

---

[2] C. Blanchett. "I believe there are some things in life you can't deny or rationalize, and [love] is one of them" [Online]. Available: http://https://quotes.ng/mobile/search/?s=%E2%80%9CI+believe+there+are+so me+things+in+life+you+can%E2%80%99t+deny+or+rationalize%2C+and+%5Blov e%5D+is+one+of+them.%E2%80%9D+Cate+Blanchett [2021, November].

strangers or acquaintances, The Almighty (God, Allah and perhaps, others) and the universe. This shall be discussed further in the next chapter, which leaves this chapter with the responsibility of discoursing the following: The main nature of love which includes Physic-emotional, Non-physic-emotional and Spiritual Natures of Love, and a Lover and a Beloved.

It is not gibberish-like to say that the first step for anyone to have a successful relationship is to know the nature of love, that is, the nature of what they feel for their partner or spouse. This is very important as it helps them to rationalise and differentiate lust from love, which in return assists them make a better choice in their relationship. It is unfortunate that some lovers may not even be able to discern what they feel for their partner or spouse but the fact that they are attracted to the person, they may conclude that it must be true love however, in the long run, they soon will realise that it is only the initial stage of love (Eros) that is playing its role. The inability to discern the nature of what one truly feels for their partner or spouse even at the initial stages of their relationship is what causes lots of heartbreaks, broken homes / relationships, love doubts, and perhaps, non-involvement in relationships. I have defined love in my introduction as a strong attraction, affection or desire towards another — implying that something brings about the attraction or affection that one feels towards another — but the basis on which this attraction or affection is felt is what most people do not get right and as a result, they tend to either love a wrong person or get loved by a wrong person. This is the reason that this chapter precedes other chapters.

If I may ask, do you know what the nature of love is? If no, do you not think that it is important to know the nature of the love that you feel for your partner or spouse? Under these circumstances, this chapter shall examine the Nature of Love and how the choice you make can affect your relationship. Basically, there are three Natures of Love, viz. Physic-emotional, Non-physic-emotional and Spiritual Natures of Love. I will take them one after the other to explain in the right proportion how you should be able to understand. But other than knowing the nature of love, it is also ideal that you know which of the sides that you belong when it comes to making your relationship thriving. I have learnt that there is a Lover and a Beloved in some romantic and marital relationships — this is really a huge determinant of some relationships — so if you do not quickly figure this out in order to strike a balance in your relationship, it may cost your relationship. This shall be discussed further after I have examined the nature of love.

The Physical and Non-physic-emotional Nature of Love

Let me guess, what pops into your mind right now is: How on earth can love be physical? It may amaze you that the first phase of love is physical and/or non-physical — the attraction and desire that you feel towards another at the initial stages are by no accident physical and/or non-physically. This is why it is imperative that I discuss the physic-emotional and non-physic-emotional natures of love that is, how love can be based on physical and/or non-physical qualities or features. Note that 'emotion' in this sense is the 'attracting factor', that is, it is the strong feeling derived from the physical and/or non-physical features or qualities of a person — it is what brings about the desire and attraction.

Physic-emotional Nature of Love

Physical denotes something that can be seen and touched, so no doubt this portion shall based on the physical features in a person that makes another person to fall in love with them or vice versa. This is not to say that what the person feels is physical but it means that the outward or physical appearance of the person brings about the attraction and desire felt by the other person — this is termed 'Eros' in Greek. According to Sarah Regan, Eros was described as the intoxicating and thrilling emotions that the initial stages of a relationship can induce, which may be as a result of the physical features that are possessed by other people. When you first meet a person, their physical features are what attracts them to you and vice versa, and sometimes, these features may have to do with lust (the urge for sexual intercourse), which is also physical however, it is not the best of the nature of love at all. You might have observed that when you meet a person for the first time, their appearance has a long way to go with the way you address and want to continue the conversation with them. You may, more often than not, cling to physical features like, facial beauty, fragrance, height, complexion, eyeballs, hairstyles, good dress sense, fame, charisma, good voice, walking steps, and other ladies and guys' physical features, this you hold to a high esteem and you may consider love until these features stop existing in them. Now, I am not exempting the physical nature of love as a means to find true love or a long-lasting relationship, of course everyone needs something that will stimulate them to take action, and more often than not humans' goals are only achieved when they have something (a motive) that inspires them but the physical nature of love may not be a means to achieving a desired relationship if you make mere physical features your priority.

Another features of the physical nature of love are material things like money, gold, diamond, platinum, to mention a few, which may be so enticing that they make you feel so attracted to a person and thus, may be mistaken for true love. Since this world has become so materialistic, it is pretty easy to meet people that you are physically attracted to and vice versa daily, but to have a long-lasting relationship, you will have to discern the true nature of what you and your partner or spouse feel for each other after you must have completely read this book.

Non-physic-emotional Nature of Love

Non-physic-emotional nature of love goes beyond the physical features of a person. Conversely to physical, non-physical are features or qualities that cannot be seen or touched but can be only felt. We all possess some attributes that are not physical thus, they cannot be seen with our naked eyes but they still make us because they contribute to our actions. These are attributes like diligence, intelligence, courage, sense of humour, mindset, belief, kindness, humility, tenderness, commitment, honesty, and other virtues, which are referred to as the inward qualities that bring about the attraction and desire felt by a person towards the other. Non-physic-emotional nature of love implies seeing beyond the physical appearance or outward of a person. That is, seeing the inside of them — the real person that they are — before falling in love with them. This, I believe is the best way to a long-lasting relationship.

Note that the initial stage of love is usually what leads to other types of love, which shall be discussed more in the next chapter.

The Spiritual Nature of Love

The Spiritual Nature of Love is simply unconditional love; it is the love that we generally feel towards every living creature around us and the universe without expecting such feeling in return — it is also known as Agape Love. What

5

makes it spiritual is because it is undiluted and unconditional, additionally, it is felt for supernatural beings and in return, humans are loved by supernatural beings. This nature of love happens to be the purest and truest as it includes loving a strange person without them having to possess our favourite features or do the things that we like. A very good example of this love for the Christians is what we feel towards the Almighty God and his mercies and compassion upon us in spite of our ungodliness and unrighteousness: "God does not want the death of the wicked but their repentance." This is the same with the love that our Muslim brothers and sisters all over the world feel towards Almighty Allah, also his love and kindness towards them in return, and likewise other religious believers.

Unconditional love is that kind of love a mother loves her children, in spite of the messes they make; children loves their mother, in spite of her tendency to nag; their father, even though he is too opinionated; we love our siblings, even though they refuse to do the house chores; our friends, even though they often forget to return what they borrow from us and also gossip; our haters, even though they never wish us well and other religious persons even though we do not practice the same religion. This is surely how we can love imperfect people perfectly, and this is the same love we expect to give ourselves!

In the Holy Bible, unconditional love is preached in a number of Bible passages, but a few of them are italicised below:

> *"Have I any pleasure at all that the wicked should die? saith the Lord GOD: and not that he should return from his ways, and live?"*
>
> (Ezekiel 18:23[3])

6

"In this was manifested the love of God toward us, because that God sent his only begotten Son into the world, that we might live through him. Herein is love, not that we loved God, but that he loved us, and sent his Son to be the propitiation for our sins. Beloved, if God so loved us, we ought also to love one another. No man hath seen God at any time. If we love one another, God dwelleth in us, and his love is perfected in us."

(1 John 4:9-12[4])

"Who shall separate us from the love of Christ? Shall tribulation, or distress, or persecution, or famine, or nakedness, or peril, or sword? Nay, in all these things we are more than conquerors through him that loved us. For I am persuaded, that neither death, nor life, nor angels, nor principalities, nor powers, nor things present, nor things to come, Nor height, nor depth, nor any other creature, shall be able to separate

---

[3] King James Version, Ezekiel 18:23, [Online]. Available: https://www.kingjamesbibleonline.org/Ezekiel-Chapter-18/#23 [2021, November].

[4] King James Version, 1 John 4:9-12, [Online]. Available: https://www.kingjamesbibleonline.org/1-John-Chapter-4/#9-12 [2021, November].

us from the love of God, which is in
Christ Jesus our Lord."

(Romans 8:35, 37-39[5])

Who Is a Lover and a Beloved?

In some romantic or marital relationships, there are Lovers and Beloved; a Lover is a person who gives more in their relationship, that is, s/he is the one that is so much interested in their partner or spouse and may do anything in order to make them happy and keep them but on the contrary, a Beloved is a person who receives the love and oftentimes are less interested in their partner or spouse thus, gives little or nothing to their partner or spouse and even make them feel shaky — giving their partner or spouse the impression that they may lose them — as if they are at stake if they do not do everything they want. These two terms are not gender-based, that is, they can be used for both male and female. The reason that some relationships crumble is because the involved Lovers fail to find out early if their Beloved really love them in the right proportion in return or not, which as a result predictably truncates their relationships when they later find out that they do not. This is consequent upon the fact that their sacrifices alone are not enough to save their relationships. The truth about relationship is that unless it is mutual, it may never work out, and let me make clear that the basis of unrequited love is a person's inability to discern at the early stage, if they are a Lover or Beloved, or perhaps in the long run in the relationship if their partner returns their love or not. It is worth bearing in mind that there is no crime in giving so much in your relationship or

---

[5] King James Version, Romans 8:35, 37 - 39, [Online]. Available: https://www.kingjamesbibleonline.org/Romans-Chapter-8/ [2021, November].

loving your partner or spouse immensely, but you have to be sure that you are not giving way too much more than your partner or spouse — you must always try to strike a balance.

The issue of a Lover and Beloved usually begins at the initial stage of a relationship when one of the involved partners or spouses possess the qualities that the other likes which must have attracted them to the person, but in contrast, they do not possess the qualities that the person likes which makes the relationship lopsided. So the one who does not possess the qualities that the other person likes becomes the Lover since they still want to keep the person because they possess the qualities that they like thus, they will be the one sacrificing more or all in the relationship in exchange for keeping them. Contrarily, the other person becomes the Beloved and will sacrifice very little or nothing because their partner or spouse does not possess the qualities that they like, as a result, they feel that they have nothing to lose. Consequent upon that, I have always advice people to "marry someone who loves them more than they love the person" I shall reiterate this statement in Chapter Twelve and explain better. Be that as it may, the below relationship experts console the Lovers with their amazing statements:

> *"The important thing was to love rather than be loved"*
> W. Somerset Maugham[6]

---

[6] W. S. Maugham, "The Important Thing" [Online]. Available: https://www.goodreads.com/quotes/225246-the-important-thing-was-to-love-rather-than-to-be [2021, November].

"If equal affection cannot be, let the more loving one be me."

W. H. Auden[7]

Although, these quotes also encourage you and your partner or spouse to strive towards loving each other equally without backing down or giving each other a reason to doubt their love. For the sake of those that do not know, I will like to state the characteristics or acts of a Lover and Beloved in a relationship. Lover: calls and texts more, gives more attention, says 'I love you' countless times, always eager to introduce their partner to friends and family, return calls and texts immediately, always thinking of how to make their partner or spouse happy, forgives them easily, says sorry even when in-culpable, prefers to lose in all fights, arguments and games and so on but on a contrary, a Beloved gives or does less of the aforementioned.

"Who, being loved, is poor?"

Oscar Wilde[8]

Well, my response to Oscar's question will be 'Yes', because Elbert says:

"The love we give away is the only love we keep."

Elbert Hubbard[9]

---

[7] W. H. Auden, "If Affection Cannot Be Equal" [Online]. Available: https://www.reddit.com/r/quotes/comments/qty6k/if_equal_affection_cannot_be_let_the_more_loving/ [2021, November].

[8] O. Wilde, 'Who, Being Loved, is Poor?" [Online]. Available: https://www.goodreads.com/quotes/1247-who-being-loved-is-poor

Additionally,

> *"You never lose by loving. You always lose by holding back."*
> <u>Barbara De Angelis</u>[10]

This is true as you may lose a good partner or spouse whom you may never be able to replace; you may as well lose all the good love and affection that they still have for you. To avoid us the chances of falling into the hands of a 'Beloved' as described in this book, and also what a 'Beloved' should do even though their partner or spouse do not possess the qualities that they want, Rambharack advises that we should:

> *"Always choose to be with someone who makes the effort to show us that we are important to them and who supports and cares for us. Lets be with someone who makes us a priority. Go for the one that loves you, don't go for the one you love, we might have to beg for their love, But the one who loves us, learn about them, invest some effort to try to really get to know them, maybe we might end up with our soul mate!!"*
> <u>Glen Rambharack</u>[11]

---

[9] E. Hubbard, "The love we give away is the only love we keep" [Online]. Available: https://www.goodreads.com/quotes/21688-the-love-we-give-away-is-the-only-love-we [2021, November].

[10] B. D. Angelis, "Never Lose By Loving" [Online]. Available: https://www.goodreads.com/quotes/412993-you-never-lose-by-loving-you-always-lose-by-holding [2021, November].

I really do agree with his advice but more often than not, when some persons are in love, they tend to conclude that their partners or spouses love them in return because they are either blindfolded by what they feel for them or they cannot stand the truth of their partners or spouses not loving them in return, so they will rather live in their delusion, but if they have to be really honest with themselves, they sure can tell that their partners or spouses do not love them as much as they do. This simply signifies that they are begging for their love while there are probably some other persons out there that would love them better. Living in delusion is worse than heartbreaks; it is ideal to face reality and graciously step out of toxic relationships.

Now, the fact about a Beloved is that since they are not interested in their partner or spouse because they do not possess the qualities that they want, they may be cheating on them with someone who possesses those qualities that they want, which leaves their partner or spouse (the Lover) nowhere in their heart. So, what is the point of a Lover living in delusion, wasting time and probably hurting? However, if we stick to Glen's advice, then there is a possibility of a Lover and Beloved still working things out and having a long-lasting relationship.

[11] G. Rambharack, "Choose Someone Who Make You a Priority" [Online]. Available:
https://www.searchquotes.com/quotation/Always_choose_to_be_with_someo ne_who_makes_the_effort_to_show_us_that_we_are_important_to_them_an d_w/496568/ [2021, November].

Chapter Two

A true relationship

Atrue relationship is the one that prevails over all the problems thereof in a relationship — not the one that does not have blemish at all or because you and your partner or spouse are perfect — of course there can never be perfect couples, but because both of you are giving your all so as to make your relationship successful. In my introduction, I mentioned the various types of love but in this chapter, I shall explain them one after the other and reveal how mistaking one for another may affect your relationship with others. This chapter shall be an advancement of the previous chapter furthermore, I shall discuss the reasons that one's relationship may never be true and how one can still make their relationship true.

Eros

According to Sarah Regan, Eros is all about romance, passion, and attraction; these are what you feel at the initial stages of a romantic relationship. It is merely to attract you and your partner to each other and does not guarantee a long term union. Like I mentioned in the Chapter One, something must have brought about the attraction that exist between two partners in a relationship — there must have been something that instigated the passion that both partners feel at the initial stages of their relationship — some of these features were also enumerated in the Chapter One, but this initial stage of love is so not enough to guarantee a true relationship, as physical features may stop existing and some feelings may die; passion may become passionless and attraction may become repulsion, however, to have a true relationship, you must know how your relationship with your partner or spouse begins, that is, what attracted you to your partner or spouse and vice versa. Additionally, you must not base your relationship on your partner's beauty.

> *"Love built on beauty, soon as beauty, dies."*
>
> <u>John Donne</u>[12]

Pragma

This is a Greek word which means 'a thing done; a fact', which can semantically be termed 'practical'. Pragma continues Eros if the love is true and not only based on the physical nature of love which peradventure brings about the attraction and desire at the initial stage. Love is practiced only when you and your partner or spouse are committed, respect each other and honest with each other; no relationship will survive if it is based on lies and/or deceits. A pragmatic love continues to exist amongst relationship's problems and survives the greatest relationship challenges. A pragmatic relationship is the one in which you and your partner or spouse keep loving each other in spite of your indifferences and looks. That is, even though either of you loses your beauty, you will keep on loving each other because what makes both of you beautiful is from within. If your relationship is not pragmatic (practical enough), it

---

[12] J. Donne, "Love built on beauty, soon as beauty, dies" [Online]. Available: <u>https://www.goodreads.com/quotes/7426096-love-built-on-beauty-soon-as-beauty-dies</u> [2021, November].

makes it apparent that it is not true; perhaps some practical qualities or actions are still missing. Note that 'pragmatic relationship' in this book signifies a relationship that the involved partners or spouses keep working tirelessly and endlessly so as to make the best of it and ensure that it last forever, in order words, it implies a long-lasting relationship.

Ludus

This is a type of love that one is not really serious about when they say or act like they love another person because it is flirtatious in nature. It is used amongst individuals who feel nothing strong or are not passionately attracted to one another. Sometimes, it is used to establish a non-romantic close relationship with a person in pursuance of making them feel safe to discuss their personal issues with them or to getting a favour from them. It may sometimes be used to lure a person into a relationship even though the person (flirt), do not really mean it. Although, we cannot conclude that a person is being flirtatious because they use words like, sweetheart, dearie, honey, darling and the likes, as these words can as well be used by parents to their children, siblings amongst themselves, close relatives, counsellors with their counselees and psychologists with their clients, but we may say that a person is flirtatious when those pet names are used to refer to them by their friends, cougar, sugar-daddy, fickle lover, crusher, etcetera and vice versa, because more often than not, those pet names are what they use to express their flirtatious feelings to each other. Some people find love in a hopeless place which implies that at times, Ludus may evolve into a romantic relationship if an individual chooses to use such strategy to get the attention of the person they are crushing on or to investigate if they feel the same way about them, but oftentimes, it is only used to tease and catch fun, it is not used with the intention to have something serious.

In conclusion, this type of love may also be referred to as 'friends with benefits' because it involves individuals who engage in a feeling that is not really serious and only for pleasure.

Agape

This word is commonly used and I want to assume that it is not new to virtually everyone. Agape is a type of love for all mankind and the universe — it is a type of love that you feel for strangers — especially people who needs assistance.

> "A purpose of human life, no matter who is controlling it, is to love whoever is around to be loved."
> Kurt Vonnegut[13]

Likewise,

> "When our community is in a state of peace, it can share that peace with neighboring communities, and so on. When we feel love and kindness towards others, it not only makes others feel loved and cared for, but it helps us also to develop inner happiness and peace."
> Dalai Lama[14]

---

[13] K. Vonnegut, Purpose of Human Life" [Online]. Available: https://www.goodreads.com/quotes/4168-a-purpose-of-human-life-no-matter-who-is-controlling [2021, November].

16

When you meet someone who is in need and distress thus, you feel pathetic for them and really craves to assist them; this should never be mistaken for a romantic relationship. Unlike Eros that can lead to Pragma, Agape should never lead to a romantic relationship which is one of the reasons that people should never love anyone out of pity. Let me cite an instance for a better comprehension: if you are working in a reputable organisation and you have a friend living in your neighbourhood who is very intelligent and diligent but struggling to make ends meet because s/he has no good job. Well, it is okay to be compassionate and always stretching out a helping hand towards those in need, and as you do that to your friend both of you are getting into each other in a long run. If at this point none of you could discern what you are feeling for each other, it may grow stronger and makes both of you want to believe that it is real love and perhaps proceed into marriage. If this happens, both of you will eventually realise your mistakes that what you felt at the initial stages was only Agape and not any of the types of love that could evolve into romantic and marital relationships. Agape love is never romantic and does not involve sex — it is one of the purest kinds of love — it does not require that a person possess the best qualities before they are shown great love.

Philia

---

14 D. Lama, "When our community is in a state of peace" [Online]. Available: https://m.facebook.com/DalaiLama/posts/10151127311192616 [2021, November].

This is a type of love that is felt amongst friends; it is a feeling of deep friendship, and also referred to as plutonic. Philia can also be mistaken for a romantic relationship if not closely investigated, as individuals can be so close that they may not be able to differentiate what they truly feel for each other. We have had people dated and/or married their friends, at times, best friends. The truth about Philia is that one may never be able to differentiate what they feel unless they have read about the various types of love and they are determined not to mix their feelings. Of course you can have a best friend regardless of their gender, but both of you mindsets really matters if you really want your feelings to remain at friendship. Certain feelings should never be muddled up with sex if they are to be experienced in their true nature, and 'Philia' is just one of them, others are Agape and Storage. When you meld any of these types of love with sex, you will never get the best of it. For instance, if you have a friend and out of the blue you start having sexual urge towards them, your mind may be stuck on this thought and until you tell the person about your libido, you may never be so free and comfortable being around them but soon as you do, if the person does not feel the same, the friendship may never be like it used to — if it survives falling apart — but if the person does, it shows that it is no more Philia. I understand that you may soliloquize right now asking: 'how about friends with benefits?' But let me clarify that if one of the benefits is sex, then both of you have taken your friendship to another level which is obviously not how a true friendship should be.

Usually, when two friends of opposite gender secretly copulates with each other, one of them is probably cheating on their partner or spouse because evidently, both of them are only seen as friends and predictably, one of them is in a relationship with someone else. One of the reasons Philia is close to a romantic relationship is that it requires virtually all the qualities of a romantic relationship: communication, commitment, honesty, caring and others, and one may also be heartbroken when they find out that their other friend betrays them or do not return the sacrifices that they make. Although, friendship has levels basically: Acquaintance and Intimacy (close and best friends). Acquaintance is a term that describes a friend that is not too close to us — we only talk to them whenever they come our ways and do not have to tell them some personal matters about us. On a contrary, Intimacy refers to the closeness of two persons; very close that we text, call and visit when we do not see or hear from them. We always try as much to keep them in close contact and check on them from time to time. In addition, we confide in them and share personal things about us with them; most of them know our deepest secrets and can tell who we are even in the dark. This is what we do with our lovers or relationship partners too but what differ Philia from romantic or marital relationship is sex! One of the reasons that friendship ends in love (romantic and/or marital relationship) but love barely ends in friendship is that once two opposite genders have sexual intercourse with each other, they have both exchanged their prides and it remains with them forever, but one of them may not feel too comfortable to have given their pride to someone they did not give their heart to and as a result, they may feel withdrawn or reluctant when they are around them except in other cases.

In conclusion, having made my point clear about Philia not being muddled up with sex, it is imperative to note that true love grows out of friendship — spending time with your potential partner or spouse in order for both of you to get to know each other better — is usually done at the friendship stages. In other ways, both of you may be friends for a long time without even thinking of dating each other nevertheless, it eventually happens. I understand that this may be the case however, it signifies that while both of you are still friends, you are sticking to your friendship and not melding it with sex, so as soon as both of you decide to take your friendship to the next level, it indicates that it is no more Philia (friendship). My conclusion is that this portion concerns itself with helping you to understand what true friendship is all about and never to be mixed up with other types of love or feelings, when this happens; it is not Philia anymore, regardless.

Philautia

This is the type of love that we feel for ourselves; it is more often than not referred to as 'self-love'. Everyone loves themselves, I guess. It is expected that before you can give love you must have it, because you cannot give what you do not have.

> *"We must be our own before we can be another's."*
> Ralph Waldo Emerson[15]

Self-love is what you feel when you eat, make yourself happy, change your wardrobe, go to the cinemas or your favourite recreation centre, get yourself nice things, prevent illness and diseases, seek for medical assistance when ill, use

---

[15] R. W. Emerson, "Be Our Own" [Online]. Available: http://https://www.goodreads.com/quotes/727948-we-must-be-our-own-before-we-can-be-another-s [2021, November].

pedestrian bridges on the roads, and take other preventive measures. If you love yourself truly, you will also be cautious of the type of person that you give your heart to or fall in love with; you will take all preventive measures and ensure that you do not fall victim of a fickle lover. On a contrary, excessive self-love may encourage you to give less in your relationship due to the fear of heartbreaks.

> *"Selfishness doesn't consist in a love to yourself, but in a big degree of such love."*
>
> Aristotle[16]

When you have such an excessive self-love that restricts you from giving adequate love to your partner or spouse and of course others, it is where selfishness emanates from according to the great philosopher; Aristotle. If you really want to have a true relationship, it is imperative that you do not let self-love get in your way of loving your partner or spouse appropriately.

Storge

This is the type of love that is felt amongst family members — it is connected by blood and close relatives. For instance, the love felt amongst father, mother, children, in-laws, cousins, nephews, aunties, uncles, grandparents, and etcetera. Now, it is clear why Storge should also not be melded with sex; it is absolutely pure in nature and should

---

[16] Aristotle, "Selfishness" [Online]. Available: https://quotefancy.com/quote/767300/Aristotle-Selfishness-doesn-t-consist-in-a-love-to-yourself-but-in-a-big-degree-of-such [2021, November].

not in any way be mistaken for romantic or marital relationship unless the family practices incest. Storge is what one feels when their kids get beaten or bullied at school and they have to go to the school on the next morning. I could recall in my primary school when my immediate older brother punched one of his friends on the face and blood started gushing out of his nose, the dude's Mum came to the school the next morning only to realise that it was his classmate who did, she then told her son to fight back next time and not come home bleeding. Storge is protective in nature but never to be mistaken for a romantic relationship.

Mania

This type of love is excessive in nature; it is experienced when a person's thoughts are dominated by someone else, that is, when the person cannot stop thinking or talking about the other person, who in most cases is their lover. Mania is mostly experienced between lovers in romantic and marital relationships, and such lovers are often characterised by clinginess and fussiness. Like I always say, "It is okay to love your partner or spouse extensively but not excessively." When it becomes excessive then it symbolises that it has exceeded the right quantity which may be a great problem in your relationship. Loving your partner or spouse in the right proportion cautions them to return the love unlike when you give love in excess and throw caution to the wind. In most cases, excessive love never sustains a relationship or makes it any better as the obsessive always put up acts like: insecurity (as a result halts the freedom of their partner or spouse), trust deficit, tempera-mentality, over-protection, overreaction, clinginess and fussiness. In my interactions with some ladies for their take on 'obsessive lovers', none of them thought that it was an ideal way of loving and none of them was willing to engage in such relationship as virtually all of them described it as a 'toxic relationship'. One of the characteristics of a toxic relationship is when the freedom of either of the partners or spouses is halted by the other, and for sure this is what an excessive lover will do to you. For reiteration, to make your relationship fruitful, you must make sure that it is well balanced up — without skewing or lopsided.

Now that you have learnt the various types of love including their functions and characteristics, it is now safe to delve into how their attributes can influence your relationship and how one or more can lead to another. This shall be expatiated in the next portion.

How to Have a True Relationship

Having learnt the true nature of love and the various types of love, it is expected that you should be able to distinguish one from the other and be sure of the specific one that you are feeling when you find yourself getting attracted to someone else. Since it has been established in this book that something is always responsible for the attraction and desire that exists between two lovers at the initial stages of their relationship which has been described as Eros, I have, however advised that you should not base your relationship on mere physical features and/or beauty.

"Love is a great beautifier."
Louisa May Alcott[17]

---

[17] L. M. Alcott, "Great Beautifier" [Online]. Available:

The truth is that if you base your romantic relationship on real love and/or non-physical nature of love, even the ugliest person will look beautiful to you regardless of how the rest of the universe sees them. It is also noteworthy to mention that feelings can evolve and lead to another, or perhaps in some cases, the feelings can be combined. For instance, since most romantic relationship starts with Eros, if it has to stand the test of time, it needs Pragma, Philia, and Storge. That is: Philia; you should make your partner or spouse your best friend, Storge; you are apparently making a family with them and, Pragma; you sure will need this in the interest of making your family stay together forever. In other case, Ludus can be combined with Agape, Philia and Philautia, but the purpose of this portion is mainly to explain how you can make your relationship real. I shall explain two basic ways to do this at the initial stages of your relationship and the 'qualities of a true relationship' might only be broached in this chapter but they shall be discussed in Chapter Ten. The two basic ways are discussed below.

Ensure That Your Partner Possess the Qualities and Features That You Really Love Not Lust

As stated in the Chapter One, romantic relationship always start as a result of a person's attraction to another person — this attraction may be based on physical and/or non-physical features — which may later evolve into marital relationship. Although, it has been advised that you should not make the physical features of your partner a priority, but

https://www.goodreads.com/quotes/52167-love-is-a-great-beautifier [2021, November].

it is never irrational to ensure that your partner possess the physical and/or non-physical qualities and features that you love. However, if a person goes into a relationship with another person because of the lust that they feel for them owing to their physical features and s/he thinks that such relationship will last forever, then they better start cutting their expectations because such relationship will only last for as long as that person maintains those physical features that lures them into the relationship. Some partners or spouses also eventually cheat while in their relationships because their other half either lost the physical features that made them get into the relationship or never possessed those features that they like. So, if you really want your relationship to be true and pragmatic, you have to ensure that your partner possess virtually all the physical and/or non-physical features that you love and help them work towards sustaining them.

One other mistake that some lovers make is that they avoid telling their partners or spouses the exact features and/or qualities in them that attracted them, but the truth is that their partners or spouses may never know this fact, thus, they may not think that it is important to work towards maintaining those features and/or qualities. Most relationships lose their flavours soon as a partner or spouse loses their cause of attraction. You should never assume or hope that your partner will change in the course of your relationship. I am going to cite an instance and will let you be the judge in the end. For instance, if a guy likes Big Beautiful Women (BBW) but the lady he is in a serious relationship with does not possess these features, and he assumes that she will get them eventually in their relationship. What condition will it leave their relationship if it does not happen? My advice for him would have been that he tells his girlfriend the truth in order to save his time and hers because I can presume that if such relationship evolves into marriage, the guy is more likely to sleep in and/or out of their matrimonial bed with a BBW who is not his wife. Similar analogy goes to a lady who likes guys with good voices and as a result, she gets into a relationship with one. What would it become of her relationship if her guy loses his voice or if she meets another guy who has a better voice than him?

Likewise, non-physical features and qualities can also take the same turn as physical features which implies that a person can also lose their non-physical qualities. For instance, if a lady goes into a relationship with a guy because of his intelligence, what happens if he loses his bearings and his senses to differentiate what is good from the other? Intelligence can also be lost especially after a brain injury or lack of use, although, recovery is possible which is why I do advise that the involved partners or spouses help each other to maintain their features and/or qualities. Additionally, if a guy loves a lady because she is caring, what happens if she stops being caring? So for reaffirmation, one of the ways to secure a true and long-lasting relationship is to ascertain that your partner or spouse possess your desired physical and/or non-physical features and qualities, and also help them work towards maintaining them so that they will not lose them. Since they possess the qualities and/or features that you yearn for, it confirms your chance of helping them to maintain them which is quite different from when they never possessed your desired features and/or qualities in the first place, leaving you with the hope that they will eventually possess them in the course of your relationship which is a wrong thing to do.

Define Your Relationships

All relationships grow in the presence of love; love is the basis on which all relationships grow out of but the type of love is what individuals must specifically define. Defining your relationship means 'to make clear' of the type of relationship that you want to establish or that you have already established with your partner and/or others. Some persons never stated clearly the type of relationship that they want with their partners or friends which leaves their friends or partners with no clue of what they really want as a result, they either give less and expect more or give little and expect so much in the relationship. Defining your relationship includes: clearing doubts and reducing expectations, discussing with your partner or spouse how you want your relationship to be, stating clearly your do's and don'ts, helping your partner or spouse to understand you and getting to understand them too and lastly, clarifying your relationship with your friends especially opposite gender friends. With all these, you can be a little certain of having a true relationship that you really seek. Some relationships get disintegrated along the line due to my speculation that either or both of the involved partners or spouses have high expectations and get disappointed because their expectations could not be met. For instance, if you are having Philia for a friend but both of you are quite close that you have the other person thinking there is more to the friendship, it will be ideal to let them know where you stand in-the-direction-to ensure that both of you are on the same page otherwise, the other fellow may keep thinking that there is more to the friendship whereas you have no such thing in mind. This will be a great disappointment to the fellow when they later find out that they are only taking the friendship too far and that their thoughts are quite different from yours. Similarly, if you are attracted to a person whom you really wish to get married to but they have no such thing in mind, although they may not know this as they cannot see through your mind, but if you can be courageous to put it straight to the person and tell them exactly how you feel about them, then it indicates that you have defined your relationship which will either make the fellow to accept your romantic or marital relationship proposal or tell you why it will not work out, however, none of you will be wasting your time. It is highly intelligent and ideal to define your relationship with your friends, partner and/or spouse, this, I believe will make your relationship real, avoid time-wasting and time-wasters.

Some relationship has come apart due to one or both of the involved individuals, partners or spouses keeping undefined friendship relationship with an opposite gender even while they are in a romantic or marital relationship. My conclusion is that, an undefined relationship will no doubt have a serious individual think more of the relationship, especially if the other fellow cares so much that they do all the amazing things that lovers do (except sex) for their friend. This may in return make their friend think that perhaps they feel something strong for them and they may decide to push their luck a little more which consequently, may put their friend's romantic or marital relationship with their partner or spouse in jeopardy. But if both friends' relationship is well defined, it will avoid the other person thinking that there may be more to their friendship and as a result, will not cause their friend's romantic or marital relationship any problems. This is the same with same gender friendship; you should always let your partner or spouse to know your friends and how your friendship with them started — you should never keep them in the dark. Lastly, you must always emphasise to your friends (especially opposite gender) that you are in a relationship (romantic or marital) as even your wedding ring do not seem to be enough to proclaim this anymore — this, I believe, will caution them from trying to push their luck. In the end, do not hesitate to tell your partner or spouse how much you love them.

Chapter Three

The Existence of True Love

There is no doubt that true love only exists in the heart of true lovers thus, the existence of true love in their hearts is what they give or share with their partners or spouses. The existence of true love in this book implies the presence of love — when love is evident in a relationship — and thus, this chapter shall examine the presence of love in a relationship; how to identify the presence of love in a relationship and the benefits of the existence of true love in a relationship while conversely, Chapter Eight will expound on the absence of love in a relationship. Without any doubts, love is a beautiful thing and its presence brings about a number of virtues that makes life easier and worth living. In fulfilment of this chapter, I shall be discussing the main characteristics of love; this is because the existence of true love induces certain virtues and/or characters that make a relationship grow stronger and stronger. Although, I may not be able to discuss them all, but the few that I shall be discussing should help you to identify others which will sure go a long way in your relationship.

To start off with, I will like to quote this, "love only exist in the heart of a true Lover." I bet the next question you may want to ask is: "Who is a true Lover?" To me, a true Lover is someone who loves their partner or spouse with virtually all the basic characteristics of true love. Certainly, people's beliefs in love differs and we all tend to love others according to our own beliefs in love, but this really do not justify a person to be a true Lover unless the person loves their partner or spouse the way they want to be loved which is termed tenderness; one of the basic characteristics of love, others include but not limited to: Great joy, Laughter and Pleasure, Forgiveness, Share and Care, Peace, Confidence and Courage, Tolerance, Grow-up Together, Patience, Trust, Practised-love and other qualities of love which shall later be discussed in the Chapter Ten of this book.

Trust
I will start my explanation with this quote:

"The best proof of love is trust."
Joyce Brothers[18]

I cannot imagine one doubting the person they claim they love — love and doubt do not blend at all. How can you think that your partner or spouse may hurt you, fraud you, kill you, cheat on you, lie to you, sneak on you, or break your heart? One of the ways to show love to your partner or spouse is by trusting them furthermore, your relationship should be built on trust. There is no better proof to showing that you love your partner or spouse other than trusting them. So, if you do not trust your partner / spouse or vice versa, your relationship will never stand the test of time, and I see no reason either of you should remain in such relationship.

Peace

---

[18] J. Brothers, "Proof of Love" [Online]. Available:
https://www.goodreads.com/quotes/105583-the-best-proof-of-love-is-trust
[2021, November].

In the presence of love, there is Peace which is the opposite of violence; the end result of any relationships where love does not exist. When there is no peace in a relationship it becomes evident that love does not exist in such relationship. Consequently, it will bring the relationship to an end in no time. There is no way possible that you and your partner or spouse will be in love and consider violence an option; both of you will rather resort to reaching a consensus.

Great Joy, Laughter and Pleasure

These three emotions are inevitable in any relationships where love exists: both lovers will derive so much pleasure in each other's companionship, they will laugh at each other's jokes (including old, silly and repeated jokes), always feel elated each time they think or talk with each other regardless of their bad moods, do crazy things as long as they make each other happy, prioritise the happiness of each other, and so on. For emphasis, these three emotions are indispensable in any relationships where love exists.

Share and Care

It is believed that, 'sharing is caring' and of course it is. We can only share things with the people we are on good terms with, those that are close to us and those we love. You and your partner or spouse should feel safe to share your top secrets with each other, share your hard times, share your materials, resources, and other things thereof to share. When you and your partner 'share' with each other, it apparently shows that both of you 'care' for each other. This is why you have to look out for these two characteristics in your relationship and if they are missing, you and your partner or spouse must work hand-in-hand towards achieving them because they are essential in true relationships. Also, do not forget that communication is one of the ways to show care and it is one of the keys to having a healthy relationship. Sharing and caring includes communication as you and your partner / spouse are communicating when you are doing either or both.

Confidence and Courage

These two virtues are not the same and are both very much needed in every relationship, especially a pragmatic one. Confidence is the feeling or belief that one can rely on their partner or spouse. You may wonder if being in love really gives confidence and of course, being in love should give you confidence; you should never be panicked of losing the person that claims they love you and vice versa, and either of you should as well have no reason to be frightened when one of you decide to check the other's devices (phone or other gadgets), discuss with each other's friends or colleagues on each other's behalf, pay each other an unannounced visit, spend a few months or years away, visit opposite gender friends, and other acts. Confidence saves you and your partner or spouse from being cynical about each other and it shows how much trust you have both developed for each other. Courage on the other hand is the ability to do what is naturally frightening but because one is in love, they may not care about the outcome of their actions. If true love exists in your relationship, you will not hesitate to protect your partner or spouse even against someone or something that is indubitably stronger or more influential than you. I will end this portion with this quote:

> *"Being deeply loved by someone gives you strength while loving someone deeply gives you courage."*
>
> <u>Lao Tzu</u>[19]

Patience

It is reputed that, 'patience is a virtue' but still, not everyone sees it this way. The truth about having a true and long-lasting relationship is that you and your partner / spouse have to be very patient with each other. Patience is a characteristic of love that both of you must look out for at the initial stages of your romantic relationship and if it is missing, you must work towards achieving it otherwise, you may not necessarily go on with the relationship. Remember: "Never assume that things would get better eventually in your relationship." The below Bible passage proves to us that:

> *"Love is always patient and kind."*
>
> <u>1 Corinthians 13:4A</u>[20]

---

[19] L. Tzu, "Being Deeply Loved Gives Strength" [Online]. Available: <u>https://www.goodreads.com/quotes/2279-being-deeply-loved-by-someone-gives-you-strength-while-loving</u> [2021, November].

[20] New International Version Bible, 1 Corinthians 13:4A. [Online]. Available: <u>https://www.biblegateway.com/passage/?search=1+Corinthians+13%3A4&version=NIV</u> [2021, November].

This is why patience is imperative in your romantic or marital relationship.

Grow-up Together

> *"You come to love not by finding the perfect person, but by seeing an imperfect person perfectly."*
>
> Sam Keen[21]

Since no one is perfect, everyone is bound to make mistakes, besides, flaws are what make all humans imperfect which are oftentimes what brings about the contentions in every relationship. One certain thing that you cannot annihilate in your relationship is 'argument' which on a bad day may lead to a brawl or domestic violence (in a marital relationship). Regardless of how much you love and understand your partner / spouse or how long you have met them, both of you will keep misunderstanding each other even as you work on your indifferences. This is the only way that both of you can learn to understand each other better and achieve a long-lasting relationship. In the same measure, Albert believes that partners or spouses must be persistent. He says:

> *"The art of love is largely the art of persistence."*
>
> Albert Ellis[22]

---

[21] S. Keen, "Love is Seeing an Imperfect Person Perfectly" [Online]. Available: https://www.goodreads.com/quotes/489333-you-come-to-love-not-by-finding-the-perfect-person [2021, November].

[22] A. Ellis, "The Art of Love" [Online]. Available:

According to Albert, the involved partners or spouses must be unabatedly involved even as they adjust and adapt to each other's imperfections in their relationships.

Practised-love (Action)

"Love is not only something you feel;
it is something you do."
David Wilkerson[23]

Similarly, Saint supports that:

"Love is shown more in deeds than in
words."
Saint Ignatius[24]

They say talk is cheap, and of course it is, isn't it? The 'freedom of speech' gives everyone the right to say whatever they like including words of deceit and as a result, it makes it possible to meet people that will tell you that they love you daily; probably because they are lustful after you or perhaps they are bored and their idle minds prompt it, while others

https://www.goodreads.com/quotes/6530572-the-art-of-love-is-largely-the-art-of-persistence [2021, November].

[23] D. Wilkerson, "Love is Something You Do" [Online]. Available: https://www.goodreads.com/quotes/814824-love-is-not-only-something-you-feel-it-is-something [2021, November].

[24] S. Ignatius, "Love is shown more in deeds than in words" [Online]. Available: https://www.goodreads.com/quotes/223712-love-is-shown-more-in-deeds-than-in-words [2021, November].

may do because they do not know the real meaning of the phrase. This brings me to my advice: unless your partner or spouse acts on their words, I can assure you that they do not love you, so I advise that you examine closely. Love is a word in action! To ascertain that true love exists in your relationship, you and your partner or spouse must practically show what you feel and say to each other — you must practically exhibit all the qualities of a true relationship that shall be discussed in Chapter Ten — only your actions should prove your words to be true. "Never fall for a person who only says but never acts towards what they say."

Forgiveness

> *"Forgiveness is the final form of love."*
>
> Reinhold Niebuhr[25]

I may have to reiterate that no one is perfect and as a result, there is never a perfect relationship. You and your partner or spouse do have your ups and downs so these are going to, at some point, cause your relationship a few hiccups and if this key attitude is missing in your relationship, it may lead to the end of your relationship. Lovers must always remember that, 'to err is human and to forgive is divine'. Of course both of you will get on each other's nerves, but you cannot possibly stay angry at the person you claim that you love and vice versa. Absolutely not! Some lovers even go as far as going to bed at night

25 R. Niebuhr, "Forgiveness" [Online]. Available: https://www.goodreads.com/quotes/267267-forgiveness-is-the-final-form-of-love [2021, November].

without making up with each other; some prefers to leave the house for days, weeks or months, while others may stop calling and/or texting each other. Some individuals can burn the candle at both ends; they may stay under the same roof with their partners or spouses and still hold grudges against them. Well, I understand that we all have our various beliefs on how to get over anger, but, have we ever thought of a better way of getting over our anger; have we tried other options thereof rather than sticking to our beliefs? Niebuhr has said it all, *"you must cultivate the heart of forgiveness when your partner or spouse wrongs you because it is the final form of love."* This should galvanise you and your partner or spouse into constant forgiveness for each other; it is what shows the level of love that you feel for each other and it comes with 'growing up' in your relationship.

In conclusion, when love is real:

> *"Love won't be tampered with, love won't go away. Push it to one side and it creeps to the other."*
> Louise Erdrich[26]

Similarly, where love exists, Saint says that:

> *"Love is the beauty of the soul."*
> Saint Augustine[27]

---

[26]L. Erdrich, "Love Won't Be Tampered With" [Online]. Available: https://www.goodreads.com/quotes/49783-love-won-t-be-tampered-with-love-won-t-go-away-push [2021, November].

[27] S. Augustine, "Beauty of the Soul" [Online]. Available: https://www.goodreads.com/quotes/24726-love-is-the-beauty-of-the-soul [2021, November].

And lastly, Zora concludes that:

"Love makes your soul crawl out from its hiding place."

<u>Zora Neale Hurston</u>[28]

Furthermore, having discussed the basic characteristics of true love, it is worth noting to mention that there are probably other characteristics of true love but the ones discussed in this chapter are only the basics — the basic characteristics that lovers must look out for perhaps, you could find more elsewhere — but you may never observe these basic characteristics in your partner or spouse if you are too obsessed with them. Obsession may make you to ignore some signs in your relationship. One of the principles to observing the existence of true love in your relationship is that, 'you must not ignore signs in your relationship'. Having learnt about the basic characteristics of true love, I expect that you should be able to easily recognise if anyone of them is missing in your relationship. If you realise this, you should not ignore and/or presume that your partner will change with time, you should also not assume that because perhaps both of you are not married yet or any other reasons that you may come up with in the interest of vindicating your partner's inability to show or practice any of the basic characteristics of true love, especially when you are blindfolded by Mania (obsessive love for their partner). Let communication be your tool for consensus and if those characteristics are still

---

[28] Z. N. Hurston, "Love makes your soul crawl out from its hiding place." [Online]. Available: https://www.goodreads.com/quotes/56210-love-makes-your-soul-crawl-out-from-its-hiding-place [2021, November].

not coming forth, then it is safe for you to exit from the relationship.

Ultimately, love may not exist in your relationship if any of the following is the reason, if: you are in love with the wrong person, either of you is not giving enough love as required, or either of you loves the other with doubts. The existence of true love is paramount in your relationship and this is what makes it essential for you to be well-acquainted with the basic characteristics of love which will assist you in the early discovery of transient relationships, and also help you work towards achieving a long-lasting relationship.

Chapter Four

Walking and Working For Love

True lovers always love in order to make the best of their relationships, but what they do to make their relationships flourish is what some other lovers may not know about and this is what this chapter stands to achieve. True lovers know what it takes to make their relationships pragmatic or long-lasting — they know virtually all the right things they need to do with respect to making their relationships healthy just the way they want them — but those who do not possess the required attributes and characteristics may either think that love is not meant for them or their partners or spouses are the bad lovers. It is noteworthy to mention that walking and working for love is not an easy task, this implies risk taking and sacrificing for love. Nassim says:

"Love without sacrifice is like theft."
Nassim Nicholas Taleb[29]

Be that as it may, it is not every lover that thinks it is necessary to risk and sacrifice in their relationship. Furthermore, Tom knows what it takes to have a long-lasting relationship and on this account he forewarns that:

---

[29] N. N. Taleb, "Sacrifice" [Online]. Available: https://www.goodreads.com/quotes/610885-love-without-sacrifice-is-like-theft [2021, November].

"Only true love can fuel the hard work that awaits you."

Tom Freston[30]

For better comprehension and indisputable facts, I shall make use of the opinions of great philosophers on love and relationships in favour of buttressing my points as it is being done in other chapters. Before you start to imagine what I mean by 'Walking' and 'Working' for love, let me explain this phrase to you. 'Walking' and 'Working' for love in this book simply symbolises the 'risks' and 'sacrifices' involved in making your relationship successful; these are the qualities I stated earlier that true lovers know about and perhaps, other lovers do not. The truth is, 'nothing good comes easy', and just like Sam Keen has stated; nobody is perfect, so you only have to see an imperfect person perfectly. This indicates that you and your partner or spouse have a lot of 'walk' and 'work' to do so as to make your relationship turn out well; the 'walk' and 'work' are termed 'risks' and 'sacrifices' in this chapter. Here is what Erica Jong has to say about walking and working for love:

"Do you want me to tell you something really subversive? Love is everything it's cracked up to be. That's why people are so cynical about it... It really is worth fighting for, being brave for, risking everything for. And the trouble is, if you don't risk anything, you risk even more."

Erica Jong[31]

---

[30] T. Freston, "Hard Work" [Online]. Available: https://www.brainyquote.com/quotes/tom_freston_532350 [2021, November].

True lovers fight for, with and by their partners or spouses in order not to lose them, in addition, they risk 'everything' for love so if you and your partner or spouse risk and fight for love, it shows how much you value each other. This takes us to Jeaneath Winterson's opinion:

"You play you win, you play you lose.
What you risk reveals what you value"
Jeanette Winterson[32]

When you and your partner or spouse tolerate each other in spite of your unruly behaviours, it reveals how much both of you value and want to keep each other. When you forgive each other in spite of the vices that both of you put up when you are with your friends or in the other's absence, at the mall, on the bus or for your inappropriate acts in general, it shows that both of you know that you are not perfect and you just have to keep tolerating each other until you finally realise your wrongdoings and adjust. Love is always a struggle; it is a battle that you and your partner / spouse keep fighting for. James Baldwin is right when he says:

"Love does not begin and end the way
we seem to think it does. Love is a battle,
love is a war; love is a growing up."
James A. Baldwin[33]

[31] E. Jong, "Love is Everything" [Online]. Available: https://www.goodreads.com/quotes/25582-do-you-want-me-to-tell-you-something-really-subversive [2021, November].

[32] J. Winterson, "What You Risk Reveals What You Value" [Online]. Available: https://www.goodreads.com/quotes/117966-you-play-you-win-you-play-you-lose-you-play [2021, November].

Real love always includes 'growing up' together and to 'grow up' with your partner or spouse, both of you must risk and sacrifice a lot in your relationship. In accordance with this claim, I concur with William Arthur's opinion which says:

> *"Love is more than a noun – it is a verb; it is more than a feeling – it is caring, sharing, helping, sacrificing."*
> William Arthur Ward[34]

It is not real love unless you make sacrifices. This chapter shall be incomplete if I do not divulge some of the acts and/or things that you need to sacrifice in order to make your relationship successful. To make your relationship efficacious, what you and your partner or spouse need to sacrifice includes but not limited to: Time, Inappropriate Acts, Resources, Beliefs, Principles, and Self-comfort and Self-pleasure. Truth is, when you and your partner / spouse truly love each other, you may not think about consequences before taking actions or you would have probably taken actions before you later realise that your actions were drastic. I will briefly explain how you can sacrifice and take risk in each of the acts of true love mooted above.

---

[33] J. A. Baldwin, "Love is a Battle" [Online]. Available: https://www.goodreads.com/quotes/1262-love-does-not-begin-and-end-the-way-we-seem [2021. November].

[34] W. A. Ward. "Love is More Than a Noun" [Online]. Available: https://quotefancy.com/quote/933983/William-Arthur-Ward-Love-is-more-than-a-noun-it-is-a-verb-it-is-more-than-a-feeling-it-is [2021, November].

Time

Antoine's opinion on one of the things that you and your partner or spouse need to risk and sacrifice for love is outrightly correct when he says:

> *"It is the time you have wasted for your rose that makes your rose so important."*
>
> <u>Antoine de Saint-Exupéry</u>[35]

Some say, 'time cost money and it is so expensive' but a lot of other people will also agree with me that 'Time' is invaluable or priceless and cannot be bought. Most of us cherish our time so much that we usually choose to spend it on valuable things especially those that generate incomes. More often than not, some persons may ignore their partners or spouses, and rather exhaust all their time on their careers, education, religions, hobbies, friends or other spheres of life that demands time and attention, exempting their partners or spouses from the list of persons that need their time and attention. Sometimes, some may think that as long as they have given their partners or spouses all the material things — especially money — that they need then that is all. This is no doubt a huge mistake if you think this way; your partner or spouse need your time and attention as much as they need all other things that make a relationship successful. Time, as a matter of fact, is an important factor that makes relationships blossom — it is what shows how much you value your partner or spouse. "Unless you have sacrificed your time for your partner or spouse, you have not loved them like you

---

[35] A. D. Saint-Exupéry, "Rose" [Online]. Available:
https://www.goodreads.com/quotes/282264-it-is-the-time-you-have-wasted-for-your-rose [2021, November].

claimed to." Additionally, you must sacrifice your time in order to make your relationship last long — in spite of how busy they get — you must make time to be with the person you claim you love because they need to share the daily happenstances and other occurrences in their day with you, share their good and bad times with you, have fun with you, plan life with you, discuss their flaws with you and also learn about yours, discuss their burdens and pains with you and so on. There are a number of reasons that our partners or spouses need our time and the list of the reasons is endless.

I could recall when I was asking my first ever girlfriend to get into a romantic relationship with me; I would go to her house after-school, but even before we started talking real well, I would go stand at the junction of the road that leads to her house and I would not leave until I see her passing by or when I am certain that she must have used a different route or means home. At times, I would stand there for hours and would not see her. That was a sacrifice I decided to make because I wanted her so bad. I believe most people must have done the same or even more than what I did back then for their partners. If you really want someone you will find it hard letting them go and even if the desired result is not coming forth, you will rather think that perhaps your sacrifices are not enough and so, you will choose to do more.

Inappropriate Acts

It is believed that, 'love changes a person', and this is true. Surprisingly, the person may not even realise that they are undergoing a change but the end result will be the only prove. Inasmuch as I have advised that you should not assume that your partner or spouse would change in due time in your relationship, I still believe that change is possible in every relationship. If you and your partner / spouse love each other as much as you both claim, you will voluntarily give up on

46

your inappropriate acts. Whatever act each of you constantly complains about the other shall be deemed inappropriate by the other and will work towards getting rid of it. If both of you really want a pragmatic or long-lasting relationship, you must sacrifice your inappropriate acts and be willing to let them go, for instance, your promiscuous and dishonest lifestyles, bad habits, late night hangouts, impatience, theft, nagging, and so on, must be capitulated. Note that the list is endless but I chose to be restricted to the mooted ones so as not to step on toes, however, inappropriate acts are relatively determined owing to the personality of our partners or spouses; what is deemed inappropriate by one may be rational to another. Be that as it may, "whatever your partner or spouse deems 'inappropriate' should be sacrificed to the extent of making your relationship get a desired result," better still, both of you should talk it out.

Resources

Other than time, there are other resources that our partners or spouses may demand from us. Basically, they are material or physical things viz. money, cars, houses, accessories, and other luxuries and emotional needs viz. kindness, care, patience, affection and others — a true lover will not hesitate to sacrifice them all for their soul-mate. We need to ensure that our partners or spouses are comfortable even though we are not — we need to learn to inconvenient ourselves for their convenience — this is one of the sacrifices that true lovers make. We must cultivate the act of deriving our happiness from our partners or spouses' happiness, that is, we only feel happy when our partners or spouses are and not until we get ourselves those beautiful cars, gigantic houses, fancy clothes, expensive jewelleries etcetera, but our happiness comes from the feeling of satisfaction, cheerfulness, joy, ecstasy, elation, exhilaration, delectation, etcetera, that our partners or spouses feel especially when we get and gift them those things. This means that we must learn to sacrifice our happiness for their happiness, and one of the ways that this can be done is when we sacrifice our resources for them.

Beliefs

Belief is the acceptance of the existence of something even without proofs. Beliefs are no doubt so strong that they sometimes impede some individuals of being in relationships with the ones that their hearts desire. More often than not, our beliefs are developed from: religions, cultures, races, genders, families, economics, education, and etcetera. To experience the existence of true love in our relationships, we may have to sacrifice some of our beliefs which might have been hindering us from giving the best of us in our relationships. If we are too stuck on our beliefs, chances are we will always argue and fight with our partners or spouses. Many times I wonder why it is almost impossible for some Muslim and Christian persons to get married. In the same way, I also wonder why some black and white persons think that they are not compatible just because of the colour of their skins, additionally, why some elite and lower classes find it pretty hard to get along, and so on — all this depends on our beliefs. "We can all live together if we sacrifice our beliefs for love." Similarly, if love exists in our hearts or relationships, we will risk going against our beliefs and break free from the bondage that restricts us from loving our partners or spouses and others out-rightly. Since beliefs make one directly or indirectly judge others, I will conclude this section with Honore's assertion below:

> *"The more one judges, the less one loves."*

Honore de Balzac[36]

Principles

Principles are fundamental assumptions or personal beliefs that guide our actions. More often than not, principles are coined from our beliefs and as a result, most people have developed their principles based on their beliefs. Personally, I live by my principles; there are certain things that I may not do if they contradict my principles, and virtually all my actions are guided by my principles. I believe that most people are like me but irrespective of what our principles are, if we really want our relationships to stand the test of time, we must either make them flexible and conducive to integrate those of our partners / spouses or sacrifice them. The first attempt may be difficult since it involves risk-taking — we will have to risk going against our principles for the first time before it becomes a repeated action. Otherwise, we may not be able to keep our principles and also keep our partners or spouses. That is why Amos 3:3 asks:

> *"Can two walk together except they be agreed?"*
>
> Amos 3:3[37]

I guess your answer is as good as mine — probably not — I do not see the possibilities of walking in the same direction with someone who chooses to walk the other way. If our

[36] H. D. Balzac, "The More One Judges, The Less One Loves" [Online]. Available: https://www.goodreads.com/quotes/27799-the-more-one-judges-the-less-one-loves [2021, November].

[37] King James Version Bible, Amos 3:3, [Online]. Available: https://kingjames.bible/Amos-3#3 [2021, November].

partners or spouses do not agree with our principles, how do we intend to work our relationships out? Trust me, if we truly love our partners or spouses, we will not see a problem in sacrificing our principles since they are probably holding us back from loving at our best; this is what makes vulnerability a sign of true love. Jane Austen says:

"To love is to burn, to be on fire."
Jane Austen[38]

Additionally, Theodore Roethke also supports my point when he concludes that:

"Love is not love until love's vulnerable."
Theodore Roethke[39]

This implies that we must risk going against our principles which makes us vulnerable notwithstanding, we just have to do so in order to make our relationships pan out well. Since vulnerability is the state of being exposed to possible harm, it is the outcome of a person who goes against their principles since it involves giving their partner or spouse the chance of hurting them. All true lovers are vulnerable; we reveal all our secrets to our partners or spouses, we trust, take risks for them and so on. All these are

[38] J. Austen, "To Love is To Burn" [Online]. Available:
https://www.goodreads.com/quotes/169182-to-love-is-to-burn-to-be-on-fire
[2021, November].

[39] T. Roethke, "Love is Vulnerable" [Online]. Available:
https://www.brainyquote.com/quotes/theodore_roethke_380699 [2021, November].

what makes us vulnerable and of course, qualifies us as true lovers.

Self-comfort and Self-pleasure

Everyone cherishes his/her comfort and pleasure, and I must say that it is one of the major reasons that people do certain things only to be comfortable. It is always difficult to put other people's comfort before ours or prioritise their pleasure over ours but in the case of true love, we must learn to sacrifice our comfort and pleasure for our partners or spouses. For instance, if our partners or spouses have to wake us up in the middle of the night to have a discussion with us, or they want us to take out the trash while we are watching our favourite shows. Sometimes, it may even be more intense like when we have to let them use our cars while we use public transport or stop seeing our best friends because they do not feel comfortable with them. The list of things that we may deny ourselves in order to satisfy our partners or spouses is endless, but with the few that are mentioned above, we should be able to identify others and work on them. Howbeit, if our partners or spouses truly love us, they will never derive pleasure in our discomfort and as a matter of fact, they will not request, accept or engage in any act that will deprive us of our comfort or expose us to danger, however, we should be ready to go to that extent if that is what it takes.

In conclusion, having discussed the risks and sacrifices involved in loving our partners or spouses immensely which also shows the existence of true love in our relationships, and having explained the types of sacrifices that we need to make in order to have a long-lasting relationship, I hope that I have been able to clarify that our level of sacrifice is what proves how much we value our partners or spouses and how long we want to be with them. The importance of sacrificing and risking for love in order to have a long-lasting relationship is that we may never in this whole wide world find people that will see 'everything' in our own way; we may never find soul-mates that share the same beliefs, principles, and habits with us, this is why it is imperative that we sacrifice those things that I may refer to as 'hindrances' in order to make our relationships successful. This may seem odd and crazy but it is expected that we do some crazy things for the sake of making our relationships prosperous, hence why Friedrich Nietzsche says that:

> "There is always some madness in love. But there is also always some reason in madness."
> <u>Friedrich Nietzsche</u>[40]

The madness in love are the crazy acts like risks taking and sacrifices that we make in our relationships, but we may not even realise our actions because we are probably blindfolded by love and as a result, our actions will seem like the best things to do. Now, where the problem lies is that after some of us might have got our partners or spouses, we tend to stop risking and sacrificing for them, we say to ourselves that: 'well, they are ours now.' Hell, no! They will not always remain ours unless we keep sacrificing and taking risks for them. May I emphasise that, "It requires more sacrifices and risks to keep our partners or spouses than it took us to get them?" If we really want our relationships to last long and be pragmatic then we must keep risking and sacrificing for our partners or spouses.

---

[40]F. Nietzsche, "Madness in Love" [Online]. Available: <u>https://www.goodreads.com/quotes/18271-there-is-always-some-madness-in-love-but-there-is</u> [2021, November].

Ultimately, inasmuch as some persons may really like to take risks and make sacrifices for their partners or spouses in order to keep their relationships on the right track, certain factors may militate against their desires and as a result, they may think that it is clever to hold back rather than being vulnerable. These factors shall be discussed in the next chapter. Enjoy reading!

Chapter Five

Why Some People Love Less

A lot of relationships have fallen apart not because the involved partners or spouses were not capable of making the best of their relationships, but because perhaps they did not think that it was necessary to know what happened in their partners or spouses' previous relationships. This is important as it helps you to understand your partner or spouse better; why they choose to love you the way they do. It cannot be gainsaid that our experiences are what shapes and reshapes our views about life and everything thereof. If your partner or spouse is acting strange in your relationship or you feel that they are holding back from loving you, there are certain things that you must find out and some of them shall be discussed in this chapter. To achieve the objective of this chapter, it is ideal that I share a few responses gotten from one of the questions in a friend's online survey and it reads: 'what would be some reasons a woman would be reluctant to fall in love with a man?' Similarly, I shall be explaining some personal reasons that I feel some partners or spouses may choose to hold back in their relationships or stop getting involved in relationships of all kinds, marital inclusive. These reasons include but not limited to: Previous Experiences, Hypo-experience, Hyper-experience, Doubts and Fear, Cynicism (lack of trust), Self-dependence, Covetousness, Egotism, amongst others. I shall briefly discuss each and every one of them.

"What would be some reasons a woman would be reluctant to fall in love with a man?"

The responses gotten from the survey includes but not limited to: **Anita B.**: *"she became fiercely independent, creating her own life and loving it... she'd enjoy some companionship but is afraid of emotions and love complicating the relationship that she is in with herself!"* **Mark D.**: *"Another way to phrase it would be, 'what are some reasons men hide their emotions and are reluctant to fall for another woman!'"* **Laurie L.**: *"Commitment issues, puts career ahead of love, parents had a bad divorce and scared it will happen to her, from an abusive home environment growing up."* **Rae M.**: *"Similar traits to someone else that she loved. Wants to focus on herself. Not sure if he is right for her and her lifestyle. Doesn't feel he is mature enough. He is love bombing (though its sincere) and she doesn't believe it genuine and views it as future abuse. She doesn't believe in love as an actually feeling because of the science behind so she isn't interested in the idea of letting hormones control her. Genuinely enjoy being single."*

Brandon R.: *"My wife said: she's been hurt by men in her past, not limited to ex-spouses or ex-lovers, but could also include male family members. Additionally, this could lessen her self-confidence and make her feel unworthy of love from any man. In general, it will be harder for her to fall in love if she hasn't taken the correct steps to heal from her past and could actually hurt any potential partner..."* **Ann M.**: *"She has been a recipient of narcissistic abusive behaviour by a former partner or husband. Unable to get over the trauma bond has PTSD and is still grieving the loss of her last love."* **Jennifer L.**: *"She's given herself over and over to a man who claimed he loved her only to be disappointed and destroyed many many times. She lost herself to the point she was totally broken into pieces that*

55

were like grains of sands. She pulled herself from the lowest point anyone could be at and she swore that she would never be out in that position again by a man or by her own subconscious actions." **Meredith P.:** *"Cultural or family pressure. In some cultures and religions, there's a lot of pressure to marry someone within the culture or religion. If there's a man outside of that culture or religion she would probably be reluctant to fall in love with them."* **Barb K.:** *"She's come out of a broken relationship and doesn't trust men in general."* to mention this few.

Previous Experiences

It is said that, 'Experience is the best teacher', and without contradictions, it sure is. As stated in the introductory paragraph above, our experiences are what shapes and reshapes our views about love (not life in this sense). If one has experienced the good side of love, they tend to love more or give the best of their love to their lover but contrarily, if they have experienced the bad side of love, they may try never to get involved in relationships anymore or they might have made up their mind to hold back in loving their partner or spouse even if they do. Nevertheless, this portion shall focus on negative experiences in relationships in order to achieve its aim. It is also said that, 'mistakes are lessons', and of course they are. If a person has experienced love negatively in their previous relationship in spite of loving their ex-partner or spouse immensely, they may regret giving them so much love and as a result, they may want to conclude that love is overrated. This may also contribute to them concluding that they should have loved with caution, but since that was not the case, they may try to avoid such recurrence thus, they may opt for loving cautiously in their subsequent relationship(s). This may be likened to what happened to me but before I carry on with my short narration,

I will like to quote Ernest Hemingway's wise words, which says:

> *"The most painful thing is losing yourself in the process of loving someone too much, and forgetting that you are special too."*
>
> Ernest Hemingway[41]

Similarly, Gugu emphasises that:

> *"Nothing hurts more than being disappointed by the one person who you thought would never hurt you."*
>
> Gugu Mofokeng[42]

These were exactly the case with me when I had my first love (the girl I talked about in the previous chapter), because I felt like it was never going to end. Also, I thought that everything was going the way it should until I realised what I did not know. By the way, that experience makes me want to suggest that it is sensible for naive lovers to be together in a relationship than being with an experienced lover; this way, both of them make fresh mistakes and it will be kind of easy for them to forgive each other unlike when one of them is more experienced (although, this is not wrong in all cases). In my own case, she was more experienced — she had

---

[41] E. Hemingway, "Losing Yourself" [Online]. Available: https://www.goodreads.com/quotes/582647-the-most-painful-thing-is-losing-yourself-in-the-process [2021, November].

[42] G. Mofokeng, "Being Disappointed" [Online]. Available: https://www.goodreads.com/quotes/10138218-nothing-hurts-more-than-being-disappointed-by-the-one-person [2021, November].

obviously been in a relationship more than once — so she could easily tell the things that I was doing wrong and she was holding back her feelings. Additionally, I was the Lover while she remained the Beloved, and I was the one making all the efforts trying to please her in order to keep the relationship going. That kept going on and on, and I kept holding on for as much that I could nonetheless, there is a limit to what every man can take or hold so predictably, I got tired of fighting alone and we parted ways since my best was obviously not good enough to keep the relationship on track; this was how I learnt that a one-sided effort may never save a relationship. After that first experience of mine, I was like: 'Is this how romantic relationship is? No it cannot be!' I refused to believe it was so, therefore I decided to try again and again, but still, they were not positive experiences. So, I chose a path to love, however, I will not treat my lover badly because of my negative past experiences in romantic relationship and I will not shut my heart from love. But Shannon Alder says:

> *"When someone you love says goodbye you can stare long and hard at the door they closed and forget to see all the doors God has open in front of you."*
> Shannon Alder[43]

This implies that negative experiences from your previous relationships may blindfold you and avoid you seeing your potential soul-mate. That is, if you decide to shut your heart on love due to your negative experience in relationship, you

---

[43] S. Alder, "Goodbye" [Online]. Available: https://www.goodreads.com/quotes/468183-when-someone-you-love-says-goodbye-you-can-stare-long?page=3 [2021, November].

may never know when you will miss the right person for you. Be that as it may, to avoid being victimised by some experienced lovers I have advised that young lovers most preferably, get into romantic relationship with novices like them because most experienced lovers may only take advantage of their inexperience since they are gullible. This is what my previous romantic relationship experiences have taught me! Nonetheless, regardless of our negative experiences in relationships, we should not desist from getting involved in new relationships and loving our partners or spouses appropriately. Furthermore, we should not victimise our new partners or spouses for the mistakes or appalling acts of our previous lovers. Henry David agrees with me when he says that:

> *"There is no remedy for love but to love more."*
>
> Henry David Thoreau[44]

Similarly, Bertrand concludes that:

> *"To fear love is to fear life, and those who fear life are already three parts dead."*
>
> Bertrand Russell[45]

---

[44] H. D. Thoreau, "Remedy For Love" [Online]. Available: https://www.goodreads.com/quotes/11123-there-is-no-remedy-for-love-but-to-love-more [2021, November].

[45] B. Russell, "To Fear Love is to Fear Life" [Online]. Available: https://www.goodreads.com/quotes/3525-to-fear-love-is-to-fear-life-and-those-who [2021, November].

Regardless of our negative experiences in our previous relationships, we still need soul-mates that will take our pains away or make them worthwhile — we need sweethearts that will make us feel that we are living again. Mahatma says:

"Where there is love there is life."
Mahatma Gandhi[46]

So, holding on to our previous negative relationship experiences and shutting our hearts on love may give us more burdens especially if we are companionless — not having partners or spouses to share things with — as such, we will have all the time to keep dwelling on the pain that our past negative relationship experiences bring us. Howbeit, when we choose to be in relationships again, we should never make our partners or spouses to feel worthless or insignificant due to our negative relationship experiences; "Everyone deserves a chance to have our true love," so we should never make our new partners or spouses suffer for the pain that our ex-lovers cause us. St. Augustine concludes that:

"Tis better to have loved and lost,
than to have never loved at all."
St. Augustine[47]

---

[46] M. Gandhi, "Where There is Love There is Life" [Online]. Available: https://www.goodreads.com/quotes/1090-where-there-is-love-there-is-life [2021, November].

[47] St. Augustine, "Better To Have Loved and Lost" [Online]. Available: https://www.goodreads.com/quotes/1946-tis-better-to-have-loved-and-lost-than-never-to [2021, November].

*Note that my suggestion for my preference of naive lovers being together in a romantic relationship than being with an experienced lover is only based on my previous romantic relationship experiences and it does not make it impeccable. Hence, this gives everyone the right to follow their heart and do what pleases them — explore your relationships with the aid of this book.

Hyper-experience

The previous portion focused on how negative experiences may give us a different perspective or belief about love, but this section shall focus on how we may hold back from loving due to our high-strung experience in love and relationship affairs. I will not be discussing much in this passage as it is one of the factors that I shall be expounding in Chapter Seven. A hyper-experienced lover in this book implies 'too much experience' or 'over experience' lover, perhaps more than it is required. These types of lovers prefer to walk gently into relationships so as to avoid being thrown out quickly. This apparently restricts them from giving their partners or spouses the best of their love. Do read Chapter Seven to find out more on how being over-experienced in relationships can restrict you from loving your partner or spouse appropriately.

Hypo-experience

This is the opposite of the previous subhead, and it denotes 'under', 'low' or 'less' experience in relationships, especially romantic relationship. In other words, a hypo-experienced lover in this book is termed 'naïve', 'novice' or 'inexperienced' lover. Some people may decide to start their love lives being careful; this may be as a result of what they have seen in movies, read in books, heard in songs or due to the experiences of the people close to them however, none of these experiences is their personal experience. Most of these types of lovers rush into relationships and as a result, may be thrown out quickly. In addition, they make lots of mistakes, they do not look out for signs in their relationships, they may not consult on their partners' actions that are not clear to them and may as well not consult before taking actions. They are also quick to exploring their relationships and loving their partners foolishly. More on this shall also be discussed in Chapter Seven.

Doubts and Fears

No one can ever love their partner or spouse wholeheartedly with either or both of these emotions; they are burdens in the hearts of true lovers which restricts them from giving the best part of them to their partners or spouses. To love your partner or spouse wholeheartedly, your mind must be free from doubts and fears of: getting hurt, losing your partner or spouse, the level of love they feel for you and so on. If you really want to love your partner or spouse with all your heart, the first thing to do is to clear your mind from all doubts and fears. Below is what Alexandra Elle has to say about uncertainty:

> *"No matter how bad you want a person, if your hearts are in two different places, you'll have to pass and move on."*
>
> Alexandra Elle[48]

Likewise, Alex Haditaghi believes that:

---

[48] A. Elle, "Hearts Apart" [Online]. Available: https://www.quoteslyfe.com/quote/No-matter-how-bad-you-want-a-1738 [2021, November].

*"Your worst battle is between what
you know and what you feel."*
Alex Haditaghi[49]

Fears and uncertainties are indubitably a hindrance to experiencing love at its best, and in this way, one can never have a long-lasting relationship. Amie Kaufman also agrees that regrets and fears contributes to us holding back from loving but here is what she advises that we do in order to overcome our regrets and fears:

*"Our regrets, our fears, they hold us
back. We have to let them go so we can
become what we're supposed to be. We
have to burn them all away."*
Amie Kaufman[50]

Cynicism (lack of trust)

A person who lacks trust for their partner or spouse will love them less. Trust is no doubt one of the key ingredients of a long-lasting relationship. If you do not trust your partner or spouse, chances are that you will be holding back in loving them. When you constantly feel that your partner or spouse: is cheating on you, does not love you, does not trust

[49] A. Haditaghi, "What You Know and What You Feel" [Online]. Available: https://www.goodreads.com/quotes/7980642-your-worst-battle-is-between-what-you-know-and-what [2021, November].

[50] A. Kaufman, "Our regrets, our fears, they hold us back. We have to let them go so we can become what we're supposed to be. We have to burn them all away" [Online]. Available: https://quotefancy.com/quote/2843032/Amie-Kaufman-Our-regrets-our-fears-they-hold-us-back-We-have-to-let-them-go-so-we-can [2021, November].

you, lies to you, is not loyal to you, does not respect you enough, keeps secrets from you and so on, then you may decide to cautiously love them; it simply means that you may be holding back your feelings. Glen posits that:

> *"A lack of trust can doom a perfectly good relationship to failure!"*
> Glen Rambharack[51]

Self-dependence

If this act is not clearly explained there is a high probability that it may be misunderstood. Self-dependence is not so wrong but when it is not well managed or controlled, it makes it difficult for a person to give the required love and affection to their partner or spouse in their relationship. When you become too self-dependent — if you can really observe yourself — you will realise that you do put up some nonchalant and unnecessary attitudes in your relationship; like holding on to little issues that you and your partner or spouse would have typically resolved in no time, and you may not even care if they tear your relationship apart. You may act this way because you have developed a mindset that portrays you can live without your partner or spouse, or you do not need nothing from them owing to your belief that you can get everything you need for yourself, but you may have forgotten that 'everybody needs somebody'.

When you are too self-dependent, you tend to care less about your emotional needs just because perhaps virtually all your physical needs have been acquired thus, you dwell more on your physical and possibly spiritual achievements,

---

[51] G. Rambharack, "Lack of Trust" [Online]. Available: https://www.searchquotes.com/quotation/A_lack_of_trust_can_doom_a_perfectly_good_relationship_to_failure%21/680115/ [2021, November].

forgetting that your emotional needs are also imperative and only a soul-mate can give you a profound emotional satisfaction. I guess that is why 'man was never created to be alone!' Being too self-dependent may avoid you doing the extras like 'risking' and 'sacrificing' in order to save your relationship. Lastly in this portion, being too self-dependent may make you want to set a standard for the type of partner or spouse that you want — having a high standard and heavy preference as criteria for the selection of a partner or spouse — this is synonymous to having a little pride. Excessive self-dependence is closely related to pride but may as well be distinctive if well managed.

Covetousness

A covetous partner or spouse is the one who is not satisfied with their partner or spouse and with the things that they provide for them. Since they are not satisfied with what their partner or spouse has or provides for them, they may consider sharing their love with someone else, which may make it difficult for them to give the best of their love to their partner or spouse. Covetousness hinders you from loving your partner or spouse wholeheartedly in the sense that irrespective of how much love and affection, and other things that they provide for you, you will never be satisfied — you may always want to cheat on them in order to make up for what you think is missing in them. Conversely, contentment is always required if you have to give the best of your love to your partner or spouse and have a thriving relationship.

Egotism

Egotism is when a partner or spouse thinks or acts selfishly with entirely their self-interest in mind. It implies that the person loves themselves too much that it affects them from loving their partner or spouse as required. Like I did explain in Chapter Two, 'excessive self-love will restrict you from loving your partner or spouse appropriately'. This is accurate with Aristotle's quote which says that, *"selfishness does not consist in a love to oneself but in a big degree of such love,"* and this is synonymous to 'excessive self-love'. Selfishness or self-interest will have you take certain actions that are only advantageous to you excluding your partner or spouse. Self-interest will make you think of yourself first in all circumstances without considering if the situation is fair to your partner or spouse. Self-interest will indubitably restrict you from loving your partner or spouse immensely.

In conclusion, if you have possessed any of the aforementioned acts, emotions and/or attributes which have possibly been restraining you from loving your partner or spouse optimally, it is a must that you work on it if you still intend to have a long-lasting relationship. For whatever reason that thwarts you from loving your partner or spouse appropriately, it will benefit you more if you let them go and work on your relationship. Holding back from loving still will not take your pain away or heal your broken heart anyway, although, you have an obligation to 'investigate the type of love' that your partner or spouse feel for you before you love them foolishly, however, you should not shut your heart on love.

Chapter Six

Love and lust: Indicators

There is no doubt that most persons especially adolescents and youths see love from a different perspective entire. As a matter of fact, most young lovers believe that if their partners avoid having sexual intercourse with them, it proves that they do not love them enough but this notion is completely erroneous, furthermore, it is misleading and disheartening. This may be the angle that John Ciardi views love when he says:

> *"Love is the word used to label the sexual excitement of the young, the habituation of the middle-aged, and the mutual dependence of the old."*
>
> John Ciardi[52]

In my own view, I believe that love is more than how John sees it therefore love must be exclusively distinguished from lust as both words are grammatically and emotionally different. This chapter shall clarify the huge differences between love and lust; it shall provide you with the indicators of lust since those of love shall be discussed in Chapter Twelve.

---

[52] J. Ciardi, "Sexual Excitement" [Online]. Available: https://www.goodreads.com/quotes/205275-love-is-the-word-used-to-label-the-sexual-excitement [2021, November].

What are lust indicators?

Lust indicators are the signs that are noticed in a lustful individual who claims to be a real lover; such signs are more obvious when the individual's interests are selfishly driven and they are what you should look out for. The signs can be attributed but not limited to the following acts: Dishonesty, Lackadaisicalness, Showiness, Suspicion, Sexual Desperation, Selfishness and etcetera. This chapter shall briefly examine these indicators, so it will be clever for you to look out for them in your potential partner or spouse's actions in order not to be victimised by a fickle lover. It is noteworthy to mention that there are other reasons that some relationships do not last long and it is not merely because either or both partners / spouses are lustful, of course some other acts also contribute to unsuccessful relationships which have been discussed in previous chapters and more also shall be examined in subsequent chapters, however, this chapter shall only focus on the lustful acts and what distinguishes them from those of true love. Although, Ralph believes that:

"All mankind love a lover."
<u>Ralph Waldo Emerson</u>[53]

And of course he is right about that, but not all mankind practices the acts of real love and not all have the intention to love their partners or spouses truly. At times, the longevity of some relationships can be determined at the early stages of the relationships based on the mindset of either or both of the involved partners or spouses. Now, that seems to be the most difficult part as humans can be so unpredictable; even

---

[53]R. W. Emerson, "All Mankind Love a Lover" [Online]. Available: <u>https://www.brainyquote.com/quotes/ralph_waldo_emerson_100714</u> [2021, November].

though a psychologist can sometimes predict a person's next move, they cannot be so sure that such person will do exactly as predicted, their prediction is only tentative so apparently you cannot know the intention or mindset of your partner, you may only predict but this chapter will assist you to virtually identify a lustful partner based on their actions. Conjecturally, I may say that a lustful partner is a person who might have also seen love from Thomas' perspective. He says:

> *"Love is a person's idea about his/her needs in other person; what you are attracted to."*
> Thomas Hobbes[54]

He may be right only if the person is lustful after their partner; a lustful person is only sexually attracted to their partner since that is obviously the major reason that they gets into the relationship. This assertion will be better understood after my brief explanations on the lust indicators that are done below.

Dishonesty

The acts of dishonesty are attributed to lies, unfaithfulness, Deviousness, Deceit, Hypocrisy, unreliability, untrustworthiness, trickiness, pretence, dissimulation, delusion and every other act that proves a person to be unreal. A lustful partner possesses all these attributes, and cannot deviate from exhibiting them to their partner. A lustful partner is pretentious; they will tell all sorts of lies about

[54] T. Hobbes, "Love is a person's idea about his/her needs in other person" [Online]. Available: https://www.azquotes.com/quote/1414167 [2021, November].

themselves, family and perhaps friends, in order to impress and to only copulate with their partner. This is why I always advice that young lovers disengage in sexual activities with their partners especially at the early stages of their relationships. I really, I am still not convinced that it is the ideal way of them showing their partner how much they love them. If your partner truly loves you, they will not hesitate to wait until you are ready for lovemaking, better still, until your honeymoon. You may save your heart from heartbreak if you are not quick to believing everything your partner tells you in the beginning of your relationship and wait until time proves it to be true. This is how you build trust for your partner since trust is always built over time. In the course of your relationship, you will discover if your partner is an honest person after you must have found out about their true intention for the relationship. If you find out that your partner has told five or six lies out of probably the ten incidents that they have shared with you, then it means that they really do not expect such relationship to last long. What do you do?

Lackadaisicalness

This is an act of showing low or no interest; lustful individuals show less or no interest in their partners' personal information, family, friends, livelihood, residence and others. They do not even remember their basic information like date of birth, hobbies, attitudes, and others. But how can they remember these when they never saved them anywhere in their diary or their long-term memory? It may be understood and pardoned if they forget a few times and you have to remind them, but if it becomes often then it makes it a little obvious that they really do not see a future for the relationship or they are probably placing a whole lot of persons or things before you. For reaffirmation, a lustful individual do not care about the types of friends you roll with, what you do for a living, where you live and perhaps, barely talk about their family or yours — they try as much to limit all conversations between both of you.

Showiness

Showiness is an act of being flashy or calling attention; a lustful person is always showy because they want to be noticed by their partner and as a result, they engage in acts like lies and pretence. Most showy partners only show off in order to get their co-partners but their acts — whatever they may be — immediately stops shortly after they must have achieved their intentions. The truth about 'true love' is that it is genuine and undiluted so you or your partner do not need to show off or lie so as to impress each other in view of getting something from each other; both of you must always appear and remain in your real selves all through your relationship. This is contrary to lust which involves pretence; trying to be whom you are not only to get your partner. But of course, showy partners or spouses know that they cannot put up their deceitful appearances forever, suffice to say, they only do that to get you and just for a short period of time. My advice is that you should cleverly avoid a showy partner because most of their kinds do not usually appear in their real selves — they are impostors and their acts are merely to get laid with you, swindle you or take other advantages of you. So, what do you do?

Suspicion

A suspicious partner is the one who expresses an act of distrust to their partner — their ways and doings are not straightforward hence, they become suspicious. When your partner gives you reasons to suspect them, for instance, uses security lock on their devices, avoids unannounced visits, avoids certain questions, never calls or texts back immediately, avoids going out with you or showing you to their family and friends, avoids receipt of calls in your presence, amongst others, you may conclude that they are not trustworthy consequently, their actions shows that they do not intend to keep the relationship for long.

Selfishness

A selfish partner is the one whose self-interest is the main reason for their decision-making and action-taking. A lustful partner is selfish if their main reason for action is only to have coitus with you regardless of how tired or stressed you are, especially when they are too eager to satisfy their sexual urge without considering if it is the right time for you or if it will satisfy yours too. They do not care if you will also enjoy the pleasure or not — all they care about is their self-interest and self-fulfilment. A lustful partner does not care about the aftermath of sexual intercourse, since they care less about your career, goal or aspiration for life. However, if a lustful partner decides to copulate with you with protections, they probably will do not because they really care about you, but because they only care for themselves (selfishness) additionally, all they care about is that one moment — during sexual intercourse. A lustful partner may copulate with you anywhere and they are always eager to take your virginity (if virgin) because they do not care about your dignity. A lustful partner is always angered when you refuse their sexual demand. All these are the attributes that are exhibited by a lustful partner.

Sexually Desperation

This section is the major reason for this chapter since it concerns itself with the sexual desire of individuals. According to Abraham Maslow's Hierarchy of Needs, 'sex' is one of the basic needs of all humans which is why virtually all individuals have sexual urge (libido) and 'sex' is the natural act needed to satisfy that urge. As a result, this stimulates some individuals, especially adolescents and youths, to engage in lustful relationships. The fact that virtually all humans need sex to satisfy their sexual urge does not make it right for anyone to delude the other to the extent of getting it from them; "Sex should be enjoyed not endured," additionally, "Sex should not be done based on delusion." It is a different feeling if one pays for sex and if one's partner willingly have sexual intercourse with them, and I am going to explain both feelings. If you pay for sex, what the fellow will benefit from the sexual act is the 'money' that they receive and apparently that is what stimulates their sexual urge; yeah, money can do that. But it will be a different feeling if you and your partner willingly make love — what both of you will derive from the sexual act is utterly and exclusively love; not personal or selfish interest. We can now read that this undiluted affection will be missing if a partner is deluded or coerced to copulate with the other.

Although, a lustful partner may want to say that since you do not know about their intention — that they deluded you — then both of you are still making love but this is not true as you may be making genuine love 'to' them owing to the fact that what you feel for them is true love yet they do not feel the same about you and as a result, the sexual pleasure is not tantamount. By the way, some of us might have seen leaked sex footages of some supposed partners on the internet. Truth be told, I have realised that most of the footages were recorded by some deceitful and lustful lovers while their deluded partners' eyes were closed as they enjoy the sweetness and pleasure of that ecstatic moment, or perhaps they were aware of the recordings but never

73

imagined their partners going to that extent since they mistook them for true lovers. In my opinion, no sane person would record their 'true lover' on camera and send the tape or file out either for money or whatever reason. This is more reason that young and gullible lovers 'must' look out for this lust indicator so as to avoid being victimised.

For the fulfilment of this chapter, let me briefly reveal how you can identify a lustful partner. A lustful partner can be identified when they are sexually desperate. A sexually desperate partner is the one who is in dire need of sex thus, throws caution to the wind for the safety of they and their partner, including other possible outcomes. How do you identify them? You will discover that all their conversations with you always end in sex in spite of how interesting they begin. In addition, sex is always their priority every time they see you. Most of them will not bother assisting you to develop and improve yourself, while very few will do that prior to the time they copulate with you after which it all stops. To holistically achieve the aim of this section, you may need to apply the principle of 'not ignoring signs in your relationship', because this will assist you to observe your partner's acts before and after both of you might have had sex. Those acts include but not limited to: beratement, inadequate or withdrawn communication, misunderstanding, impatience, inadequate visitation and care, irascibleness and others.

In conclusion, it is worth noting that a 'true lover' will never engage in any of the aforementioned acts in order to get their potential partner or spouse neither will a true partner or spouse who is willing to have a long-lasting relationship commit any of them. It is also notable to emphasise that the longevity of every relationship strictly lies on the mindsets and actions of the involved partners or spouses. If you or your partner or spouse has a lustful mindset, and act towards it exhibiting any of the indicators as explained in this chapter, this may see your relationship hit a dead-end in no time. In other case but rarely, one of you may use your unending love to change the mindset of the other and your relationship may survive. Find out what the next chapter has to unravel about an experienced lover. Cheers!

Chapter Seven

An experienced lover

I have stated in my introduction that 'love is practical', which implies that in spite of what we read or hear about it, it should not make us good or bad lovers, and it absolutely will not guarantee us a utopian relationship. For reiteration, reading books and/or watching movies will not make us experienced lovers, they may only make us cautious of loving our partners or spouses which may in return positively impact or negatively influence our relationships. On this account, this chapter shall briefly distinguish between a bookish-lover and an experienced lover. It shall also examine a few advantages and disadvantages of being an experienced lover but first, we need to know who experienced and bookish lovers are.

Who are experienced and bookish lovers?

'Experience' is in other words is termed 'undergo', 'pass through', 'contact with', 'involvement in', 'participation in' and etcetera, which implies that a person is personally involved in an event or occurrence. On this account, an experienced lover is any individual who has accumulated experiences as a result of their involvement in their previous relationship(s); the occurrences in their previous relationship(s) are what make them an experienced lover. Contrarily, a bookish-lover in this book is not merely a bibliophile but it is defined as a person who reads more of romance novels in order to learn about love and relationships, that is, their knowledge about love and relationships is based on other people's experiences, not theirs. Well, you may want to argue that this is a better way to learn about love and relationships since the individual gets to acquire more knowledge from numerous experienced lovers however, this is not the best way to learn about love. This Iris' quote below agrees with my opinion:

> *"We can only learn to love by loving."*
>
> Iris Murdoch[55]

This is true as every individual has different experiences when they engage in romantic or marital relationship. Individuals' experiences really vary as all humans possess different traits, aptitudes, attitudes, and attributes. Humans' beliefs also vary, so the way each individual will treat their partner will definitely vary. If a bookworm reads a story about an author who has experienced good loving or if the author has based their story on the successes of a protagonist's relationship, such person may not learn about 'relationship conflicts' from the author's experience as they will never learn about the little or big fights and arguments that the person (author or protagonist) must have handled intelligently and since the experience that they acquire from the individual is inadequate, it will not guarantee them of having the same experience in their relationship. Similarly, if a bookworm reads about a lover who has experienced a bad relationship, it does not mean that they have learnt about all the acts that probably made such relationship bad, neither does it thwart them from having a long-lasting relationship.

---

[55] I. Murdoch, "Love by Loving" [Online]. Available: https://www.goodreads.com/quotes/58682-we-can-only-learn-to-love-by-loving [2021, November].

So, I will conclude with Iris' quote that: *"One can only learn to love by loving."*

Having distinguished between an experienced and bookish-lover let me explicate a few advantages and disadvantages of an experienced lover. It has been defined earlier that an experienced lover is a person who must have been through a relationship to have accumulated their experience, this can in order words be described as the lessons learnt from their previous relationship or relationships, which may either deprive them from loving or assist them to love their partner better as discussed in Chapter Five but for the attainment of this chapter, I shall discuss the advantages of being an experienced lover which are: Relationship Improvement and Cautious Loving, and the disadvantages: Cautious Loving and Pride. In my discussion below, you may be amazed to know that it is not every individual who has had a romantic relationship allows their previous experiences to influence their subsequent relationship and you will also learn that cautious loving can be advantageous and disadvantageous.

Advantage: Relationship Improvement

Like I have briefly stated above, it is not everyone who has been through a romantic relationship once or more allows their previous experiences to thwart them from loving their partner appropriately in their present or subsequent relationship. Having stated this, Chapter Five explains that individual's relationship experience differs; some are inexperienced or experienced while others have positive experiences or negative experiences but whatever the case may be, the person sees the good side of their experiences instead and use the lessons learnt from their previous relationship(s) to improve their next relationship. For instance, if a lady's partner cheated on her in her previous relationship which leads to their breakup, but instead of being distrustful of her partner in her subsequent relationship, she tries finding out why her ex-boyfriend cheated on her and when she finds out what was missing in her previous relationship which she believes could have been the reason that her ex-boyfriend cheated, she tries to adjust in her subsequent relationship. This is one of the advantages of being an experienced lover — it makes room for self-adjustment and contributes to relationship improvement.

Advantage: Cautious Loving

A cautious lover in most cases is an experienced lover. More often than not, they are the one who makes use of their previous relationship experiences as a guide in their subsequent relationship(s). This kind of partner do not throw caution to the wind when loving because having experienced one or more of the lustful indicators in their previous relationship(s) as discussed in Chapter Six, they will avoid letting such occurrence to repeat itself in their next relationship. The benefits of this are: it saves you from heartbreak, it helps you to discern the lust indicators and consequently, saves you from having to deal with a lustful partner all over again, it avoids you allotting regrets and blames to yourself and/or others, it helps you in making a good selection of your partner or spouse, it helps you in good decision-making in your relationship, it helps you not to give too much affection more than you receive from your partner or spouse that is, being a Lover as discussed in Chapter One, amongst others. Although, being cautious has been explained to be advantageous in this section, but it also has its disadvantages which shall be expounded in the next section.

Disadvantage: Cautious Loving

A cautious lover in this sense is a person who is careful of their emotions thus, restricts them from giving the best of their love to their partner. A cautious lover may otherwise, hold back their feelings because they do not want to be hurt again or have a cause to regret giving so much. This is why Douglas says:

> *"People who are sensible about love are incapable of it."*
>
> <u>Douglas Yates</u>[56]

In accordance with Douglas' opinion, they are incapable of love because they are restricted in loving, that is, they do not love with all their heart. I understand that it is contentious to say that, 'the best way to love is to love foolishly', which implies that one needs to love their partner as if heartbreak, unfaithfulness, dishonesty, and/or other relationship issues do not exist. In my opinion, this seems to be the way to experience love at its best, however it sure has its disadvantages too. Usually, our first love always happens to be the best; this is so because both partners are young and insensible of love, does not know about the risks involved in their actions, well, they do not even know if there is one, all they do is give the best of their love as pure and natural as it is to each other because they are not cautiously loving each other. Now, loving foolishly does not signify that you are foolish but rather, it is the things that you do out of love that may seem foolish and not you as a person, as it is of those foolish things that wisdom is born as agrees by Marty:

---

[56] D. Yates, "Sensible About Love" [Online]. Available: https://www.goodreads.com/quotes/94945-people-who-are-sensible-about-love-are-incapable-of-it [2021, November].

*"Wisdom is born of the foolish things
one does for love."*

Marty Rubin[57]

For instance, it seems foolish to forgive your partner and accept them back in spite of them cheating on you, it may seem foolish to travel a million miles only to see your partner, or does it not seem foolish for you to completely trust your partner whom you have only met? But all these are completely wise if done out of love. Well, you will agree with me that the feelings of true love are overwhelming and thus cannot be controlled because love is not something that we can control — true feelings are way out of our control. On this note, Paulo believes that:

"Love is an untamed force. When we try to control it, it destroys us. When we try to imprison it, it enslaves us. When we try to understand it, it leaves us feeling lost and confused."

Paulo Coelho[58]

According to Paulo, a cautious lover may be confused, lost, enslaved and destroyed if they hold back in their relationship. Suffice to say, being a cautious lover may restrict you from loving your partner or spouse appropriately

---

[57] M. Rubin, "Foolish Things" [Online]. Available:
http://www.99stuffs.com/quote/wisdom-born-foolish-things-one.html [2021, November].

[58] P. Coelho, "Untamed Force" [Online]. Available:
https://www.goodreads.com/quotes/70588-love-is-an-untamed-force-when-we-try-to-control [2021, November].

and as a result, may hinder you from making your relationship worth its weight in gold.

Disadvantage: Pride

Pride has been described as an act that is closely related to excessive self-dependence in Chapter Five. Similarly, it has been established that being too self-dependent may make you want to set a standard as regards the type of partner or spouse that you want, and this is what this segment will shed light into. Pride will make you build your wall so high that a common person — who probably would have been your soul-mate — will not be able to climb. When you set a high standard, your pride also goes up with it so you are never going to settle for anything less which is contrary to the characteristics of 'unconditional love' that establishes that you must love your partner or spouse without them having to possess equal or better achievements than you. Pride will not make you realise your mistakes and thus, you will not see a reason to apologise for your wrongdoings in your relationship. Nevertheless, do not get it twisted, Pride is good but when it is excessive or mishandled it may become a hindrance to one's love life or relationship success.

In conclusion, having examined who an experienced lover is, I have not adjudged that you must be an experienced lover or not in order to make your relationship successful, but I have given both the advantages and disadvantages of an experienced lover which leaves the ball in your court. However, I will like to make this clear that irrespective of the number of books that you might have read or shall read, or the heap of movies that you have watched or shall watch about love and relationships, they will never make you an experienced lover; this can only be made when you fall in love and get into a romantic or marital relationship. Being an experienced lover may assist you in having a long-lasting relationship and may as well deprive you of such; this is the choice that you have to make. What do you do?

Chapter Eight

Faded Love and Relationship Issues

The dictionary meanings of the word 'fade' includes: 'to grow weak', 'to lose strength', 'to decay', 'to perish gradually', 'to wither', 'to sink away', 'to grow dim', 'to vanish', 'to lose freshness, colour or brightness', 'to become faint', etcetera. Now, according to these definitions, a faded love will imply a romantic or marital relationship that is experiencing one or more of the above descriptions but unfortunately, some lovers do not even know when their relationships are losing their freshness and brightness. All relationships happen to be very strong and bright at the early stages but not all relationships will maintain the good qualities that they started off with for a long time, that is, not all romantic and marital relationships will become pragmatic and several reasons for this have been discussed in the previous chapters. Although, some acts are deliberate while others are not, but if you are certain that your acts or those of your partner or spouse are not intentional, the next step is for you to look out for 'the signs that show that your relationship is fading away' with a view to assist you to fight back and make your relationship strong like it began.

This chapter shall examine ''the signs that show that your relationship is losing its strength'' and after these signs must have been discussed, a few advice shall be suggested in order to assist you to get your relationship back on track. For an in-depth knowledge, I will briefly discuss some reasons that love fades after which I will also examine the signs that prove that your love or that of your partner or spouse is fading away. Anais finds that:

> *"Love never dies a natural death. It dies because we don't know how to replenish its source. It dies of betrayals. It dies of illness and wounds; it dies of weariness, of witherings, of tarnishings."*
>
> <u>Anais Nin</u>[59]

Anais' reasons that love fades and/or dies are true as some people fail to persistently pitch-in so much efforts into their relationships like they did before they began and just like I stated in Chapter Four and I quote again: "It requires more sacrifices and risks to keep your partner or spouse than it took you to get them." How do you do this? Both of you have to keep being yourselves: dress good like always, remind yourselves of how beautiful or handsome you are, keep up with the good communication, care, understanding, and also encouraging each other to get better. Now, when either or both of you fail to do all these, thence is where: betrayals, illnesses, wounds, weariness, witherings and tarnishings originate from, according to the Anais. For emphasis, when you and/or your partner / spouse fail to persistently do the aforementioned, the love in your relationship will start fading and your interests will start diminishing. This can be likened to a farmer who strives to get a capital, a piece of land, farm implements, seeds and/or seedlings, and compost. Afterwards, s/he extirpates the

---

[59] A. Nin, "Love Never Dies a Natural Death" [Online]. Available: <u>https://www.goodreads.com/quotes/777-love-never-dies-a-natural-death-it-dies-because-we</u> [2021, November].

grasses and weeds on the piece of land and decides to sow on it, but fail to water their crops after planting. I bet you can tell what is expected of the crops and in equal measure it is the probable outcome of a relationship that its source is not replenished.

Having discussed the reasons that some relationships fail, let me further discuss the signs that prove that the love in one's relationship is fading away some of which shall be discussed while others shall be referenced if already discussed in any of the previous chapters or in subsequent chapters. These signs include but not limited to: Apathy, Inadequate Communication, Inadequate Care, Lack of Understanding, Dishonesty (Read Chapter Six), Inadequate Patience, Malice and Lack of Forgiveness, Secrecy, Pride and Disrespect, Selfishness (Read Chapter Six), Inadequate Attention, amongst others.

Apathy

Apathy is simply lack of interest, emotion, motivation or enthusiasm — it is when one's partner or spouse shows less interest in the things that they used to crave and ask for. For instance, if your partner or spouse gets peeved when you do not call, text or visit them but suddenly they decide not to care if you do or not — they do not worry about it no more — it shows that their zeal to see and/or hear from you has attenuated thus, they are not bothered if you get in touch or not. This is a very good instance of apathy. Steve's opinion on the signs that indicate that one's relationship has lost its freshness is not different from mine when he says:

"Being close but feeling far, talking but not being heard, loving but not being loved, that is the painful reality of a dying relationship."

Steve's belief also identifies apathy as an indicator that shows that one's relationship is growing weak. Apathy, of course, leads to other factors which shall be subsequently discussed in this chapter.

Inadequate Communication

Communication is indubitably the major element in every successful relationship. The role of communication in a long-lasting relationship cannot be overemphasised. Accordingly, experiences and books have proven this to be true as no relationship can flourish if it lacks communication or when it is inadequate. It is with the aid of communication that you and your partner or spouse discuss the issues in your relationship and reach a common ground. Similarly, when either or both of you is emotionally and/or psychologically perturbed, it eases your worries when you both discuss them with the other and when you both listen to each other, suggest some possible solutions and console each other. But when either of you refuses to answer each other's calls, text each other back, spend some time with each other, listen to each other and etcetera, like you both used to then you may start to worry about your relationship — it may be that your relationship is sinking away.

Inadequate Care

To care about someone means to worry or be concerned about them thus, a caring partner or spouse possesses acts like worrisomeness, anxiousness and fussiness. So when

[60] S. Maraboli, "Painful Reality of a Dying Relationship" [Online]. Available: https://www.goodreads.com/quotes/593856-being-close-but-feeling-far-talking-but-not-being-heard [2021, November].

your partner or spouse stops worrying about certain things about you like, your wellbeing, safety, emotions, self-improvement, future, family and friends, etcetera, then you can be almost certain that your relationship is losing its strength. For instance, if your partner or spouse is the type that cannot bear not seeing you three or four times in a week and also cannot do without checking up on you daily, but they suddenly stop doing all that without a genuine reason, then you may conclude that your relationship is fainting.

Lack of Understanding

Every good lover can attest to the importance of 'understanding' in a relationship just like communication. Understanding is defined as the emotional process of comprehension and assimilation of knowledge, in other words, it is the ability to have a solid grasp of an occurrence or situation. Understanding in a relationship is when the involved partners or spouses see things in each other's perspective, that is, it helps the involved partners or spouses to grasp the reason that either of them takes certain actions even without the consent of the other and as a result, reduces their level of anger to the barest minimum. Since understanding helps you to identify the reasons that your partner or spouse may take some actions, you may not necessarily hold their actions against them. But contrary to the positive side, if 'understanding' is missing in your relationship, you and your partner or spouse will always end up fighting in every argument which is a sign that the love in your relationship is fading off. If your partner or spouse has always been the one showing 'understanding' even when you are wrong, but suddenly refuses to see things your way, then you may start to think that love is vanishing in your relationship.

Inadequate Patience

There is practically no relationship that will survive without patience; this is an act of waiting without one losing their temper or getting angry. When a relationship is still fresh, the involved partners or spouses tend to exercise patience and tolerate each other but if something goes wrong in their relationship, either or both of them tend to lose patience easily and act imprudently — they become impulsive. For instance, if your partner or spouse can wait for you till forever without getting exasperated or displeased if both of you are to meet up for a rendezvous or tryst but later in your relationship, they suddenly cannot bear waiting for a few minutes before getting annoyed then it shows that the love in your relationship is not as strong as it used to. Similarly, if your partner or spouse suddenly start acting sternly in every discussion without even allowing you to explain the reason for your actions or perhaps when both of you have a misunderstanding and one or both of you refuses to take a deep breath before taking actions. If this persists in the relationship then you may start to think that your relationship is sinking away.

Malice and Lack of Forgiveness

Forgiveness is an act of letting go of any negative feelings or desires for punishment or retaliation. According to Reinhold, forgiveness has been found to be the final form of love. Clearly, this will not be the one time I will state in this book that "there is no perfect relationship" and as a result, you and your partner or spouse are bound to infuriate each other either intentionally or not, but what matters most is your persistence to forgive each other's imperfections without keeping malice or grudges against each other. Forgiveness must be absolute in a true and long-lasting relationship but when you or your partner / spouse suddenly start holding grudges and act strangely when an inappropriate act is committed by the other, then that will apparently deprive you from loving each other optimally and as a result, it will diminish the love in your relationship, suffice to say, your relationship is withering. When either or both of you start finding it difficult to forgive each other then it implies that the love in your relationship is getting feeble. What do you do?

Secrecy

This is an act of keeping secret; it is a hidden knowledge with the intention to make the deed unrevealed or undisclosed. Secrecy considered being the opposite of transparency and it is never a good act in a relationship. However, secrets really are only told to the people that we love and trust because we believe that they will never reveal what we tell them to anyone, so if either or both partners or spouses keep secrets from the other, it shows that they do not trust each other well enough and for this reason, they do not love each other enough. In a relationship where love is at its best, secret becomes a misdeed between the involved partners or spouses and in actual fact, none of them will consider it an option because they see themselves as each other's motivator, problem solver, counsellor, psychologist, consoler, companion, etcetera, and they believe telling each other about their worries and problems will alleviate them even though they cannot always be prevented. Otherwise, when a secret is leaked, it implies that the 'sly' has been keeping the knowledge from their partner or spouse for a while which would make it painful to the other person having been kept in the dark ever since the deed has been done. When you or your partner / spouse start to consider secrecy an option for whatever reason in your relationship, it indicates that the light in your relationship is growing dim.

Pride and Disrespect

Pride is the state of being proud; it is an act of an unreasonable overestimation of a partner's own superiority in talents, beauty, wealth, rank, achievements etcetera, while disrespect is simply a lack of respect; it is when a partner or spouse lacks respect for the other. Pride in a romantic or marital relationship does not enable a partner or spouse to mea culpa, be submissive, apologetic or remorseful, appreciative, which may as well lead to being disrespectful to their co-partner or -spouse. When your partner or spouse start taking certain actions persistently without consulting you and still does not think that it is necessary to apologise afterwards, then you are not being pessimistic to think that the love in your relationship is growing weak. When you and your partner / spouse start finding it difficult to respect and be submissive to each other, then apparently the love in your relationship is vanishing.

Inadequate attention

Attention is simply a mental focus; it is an act of expressing concern for or interest in someone or something. In my opinion, I feel that: *"Where there is no attention, there cannot be communication."* Of course, this is true because without a partner or spouse listening while the other is talking then everything either of them says shall be futile. Every relationship requires that the involved partners or spouses pay close attention to each other when they are in need. This helps the one sharing their worries and pains to be more comfortable and optimistic that their distress shall vanish, and of course, it eases them when their thoughts are heard unlike when they try to share their problems and their partner or spouse gets busy with something else and not paying attention which may make them feel like they are in their problems alone. When your partner or spouse start denying you of their attention, it is not unreasonable to conclude that the love in your relationship is perishing gradually.

In conclusion, having discussed the reasons that some relationships do not stand the test of time and the signs that prove that the love in one's relationship is fading away, it is ideal to advise that you can only save your relationship if you pay close attention to the aforementioned and discussed signs, and talk them out with your partner or spouse if you still want your relationship to flourish. But if your partner or spouse still will not like to do the necessary things then it is okay for you to let them go. Washington says that:

> *"Love is never lost. If not reciprocated, it will flow back and soften and purify the heart."*
> <u>Washington Irving</u>[61]

On this note, I come to a conclusion on this chapter and shall examine love in its truest and purest forms in the next chapter. Enjoy reading!

---

[61] W. Irving, "Love is Never Lost" [Online]. Available: https://www.goodreads.com/quotes/48538-love-is-never-lost-if-not-reciprocated-it-will-flow [2021, November].

Chapter Nine

The Truest and Purest Forms of Love

Love is indubitably the most amazing and wonderful thing, but unfortunately, it has been labelled some bad names based on how some persons see it. The Truest and Purest Forms of Love simply means 'love at its best', that is, 'how love is supposed to be'. It is rumoured that, 'love makes the world go around', and perhaps it does. I must have briefly discussed 'true love' in Chapters One and Two of this book, but in this Chapter I shall copiously examine love in its truest and purest forms using the opinions of great philosophers and love experts as it has been done in the previous chapters. Similarly, this chapter shall dig into the characteristics of true and pure love. I assume that you will not contend with me to say that true and pure love only exist in the heart of a true and pure individual. The Truest and Purest Forms of Love are characterized by but not limited to: Un-conditionality, Un-boastfulness, Un-deceitfulness, Freedom, Holiness, Unreasonableness and Foolishness, Desire (hunger), Unselfishness, Tolerance, Care, etcetera. I shall be restricted to these few in my discussions so as to avoid a lengthy and superfluous book.

Love is amazing and wonderful but a blemish love is never so, which is why this chapter is written with a view to helping you achieve the truest and purest love that can only be obtained by a truest and purest heart. Jiddu affirms that:

"The moment you have in your heart
this extraordinary thing called love and

93

feel the depth, the delight, the ecstasy of it, you will discover that for you the world is transformed."

Jiddu Krishnamurti[62]

The first characteristic that I shall be discussing in this chapter is love that is unconditional.

Un-conditionality

This has been discussed in Chapter One and it is expounded to be the best of love because of its nature of loving a person in spite of their bad characters or traits. Unconditional love is absolute; it is without conditions, limitations, reservations or qualifications of any kinds. It is the type of love that you feel for your partner or spouse without them having to possess equal or better achievements than you. The real practice of unconditional love is quoted below:

"Love is always patient and kind. It is never jealous. Love is never boastful or conceited. It is never rude or selfish. It does not take offense and is not resentful. Love takes no pleasure in other people's sins, but delights in the truth. It is always ready to excuse, to trust, to hope, and to endure whatever comes."

1 Corinthians 13:4-7[63]

---

[62] J. Krishnamurti, "Extraordinary Thing" [Online]. Available: https://www.brainyquote.com/quotes/jiddu_krishnamurti_100724 [2021, November].

[63] New International Version Bible, 1 Corinthians 13:4-7. [Online]. Available: https://www.biblegateway.com/passage/?search=1+Corinthians+13%3A4-

Additionally, Madonna supports these statements when she says:

> "To be brave is to love someone unconditionally, without expecting anything in return."

To love your partner or spouse unconditional is to expect nothing from them in return — loving them without benefits or having them do nothing for you in return. Unconditional love affords you to love your partner or spouse for whom they are without expecting them to be perfect. This is indubitably one of the truest and purest forms of love and to make your relationship pragmatic, you and your partner or spouse must practice its characteristics in your relationship.

Unreasonableness and Foolishness

To love your partner or spouse truly and purely which has been characterized by unconditional love, you may seem to be like a fool. Think of it, you may ask yourself: why do I need to love someone who is not in my league? Why should I love someone who is poor? Why should I love someone who is diseased? Why should I love a Christian, Muslim or other believers? Why should I love an older or younger person? And so on. But a true and pure love will make you do things that you and/or other persons may see as foolish or unreasonable. Matt also agrees that:

7&version=NIV [2021, November].

[64] Madonna, "Unconditional" [Online]. Available: https://www.goodreads.com/quotes/123182-to-be-brave-is-to-love-someone-unconditionally-without-expecting [2021, November].

"Unconditional love is quite foolish, but it is the only kind of love that can change the world."

Matt Tullos[65]

Un-boastfulness

I will begin this section with the below amazing Bible verse:

"Love is never boastful or conceited."

1 Corinthians 13:4C[66]

True and pure love does not encourage you to brag about your achievements to your partner or spouse, as this may make them feel worthless or inferior. Being boastful about your achievements to your partner or spouse may have them feel worthless especially if they are not of the same league with you. Consequently, they may see it as a scornful expression and thus, see you as a supercilious, condescending person. A true and pure lover does not brag about their achievements to their partner or spouse but rather, they either see the possibility of their achievements as a combined effort with their partner or spouse or however, they act modestly or humbly before them.

Un-deceitfulness

---

[65] M. Tullos, "Unconditional Love is Quite Foolish" [Online]. Available: https://www.wisefamousquotes.com/matt-tullos-quotes/unconditional-love-is-quite-foolish-but-it-is-218795/ [2021, November].

[66] New International Version Bible, 1 Corinthians 13:4-7. [Online]. Available: https://www.biblegateway.com/passage/?search=1+Corinthians+13%3A4&version=NIV [2021, November].

A deceitful lover has been discussed in Chapter Six; which clearly distinguishes a real lover from a lustful partner, suffice to say, true and pure love does not take kindly to deceitfulness. This beautiful quote below says:

> *"Love is many things, but it is never deceitful. Nothing toxic comes from genuine love. Remember that."*
>
> Joseph T.[67]

A true and pure love does not accommodate deception; 'you do not have to delude your partner or spouse in order to make them love you.' True and pure love interdicts pretence, lies, coercion and delusion.

Freedom

When you are in a relationship where you and your partner or spouse share true and pure love then both of you should be free and never restricted — true and pure love gives room for freedom. This portion encourages you and your partner or spouse not to make each other feel like you are in a prison in your relationship. Since true and pure love forbids doubts and dishonesty, you and your partner or spouse should never have a reason to feel insecure about each other likewise, neither of you should restrict the other of their activities. A true and pure love must take kindly to freedom of speech, movement, lifestyle, relationship, hobby etcetera, and also help you and your partner or spouse to improve each other.

---

[67] T. Joseph, "Nothing Toxic Comes From Genuine Love" [Online]. Available: https://www.pinterest.com/pin/627830004277732503/ [2021, November].

"One word Frees us of all the weight
and pain of life: That word is love."

Sophocles[68]

Similarly, Johann agrees that:

"Love does not dominate; it
cultivates."

Johann Wolfgang von Goethe[69]

Holiness

When something is holy it symbolises that it is clean, pure, and without blemish — flawless. Marilynne says that:

"Love is holy because it is like grace
– the worthiness of its object is never
really what matters."

Marilynne Robinson[70]

Love is perfect! Although, lovers are not perfect because there is absolutely no perfect person on earth however, what we feel for our partners or spouses can be close to perfect since love has its ways of making a couple perfect for each

---

[68] Sophocles, "One Word Frees Us All" [Online]. Available: https://www.goodreads.com/quotes/277213-one-word-frees-us-of-all-the-weight-and-pain [2021, November].

[69] J. W. V. Goethe, "Love Does Not Dominate" [Online]. Available: https://www.goodreads.com/quotes/179703-love-does-not-dominate-it-cultivates [February, 2022].

[70] M. Robinson, Love is Holy" [Online]. Available: https://www.goodreads.com/quotes/316327-love-is-holy-because-it-is-like-grace--the-worthiness-of [2021, November].

other; this is a process of adjusting, readjusting and adapting to each other's discrepancies or imperfections. You and your partner or spouse may not be perfect, but love is always perfect! Likewise, a true and pure love must be genuine and holy! True and pure love is holy because it is patient, honest, humble, understanding, tolerating, caring, unconditional, and including all other characteristics. True and pure love is also holy in the sense that it does not tolerate cheating, adultery, dishonesty, pride, and other inappropriate acts that oppose genuine love. It is up to you and your partner or spouse to make your relationship 'holy'.

Desire (hunger)

To desire for someone or something means to have a strong feeling of wanting or wishing to have them earnestly. Diogenes says:

"Love comes with hunger."

Diogenes[71]

Of course, it comes with hunger — having a strong desire or craving for someone or something. If you and your partner or spouse feel true and pure love for each other, both of you will have the desire to speak and listen to each other every time; give each other your undivided attention and care, meet, assist and improve each other — you will constantly think of how to make each other better. Needless to say, I understand that one more thing that you will desire for is sex since it is one of the humans' basic needs. Howbeit, in my opinion, sex should only be done by life-partners or -spouses because it is

---

[71] Diogenes, "Love Comes With Hunger" [Online]. Available: https://www.quotemaster.org/q8ab13791ec3032a5c7fd4b75afd8c9c2 [2021, November].

99

a covenant that binds both of them together by blood. Sex is when your body and soul becomes one with that of your partner or spouse which is why it is ideal and advisable to only have sex with your lifetime partner or spouse — your sexual desire should always drive you and your partner or spouse to each other rather than to your fickle lover or sexual partner.

Unselfishness

True and pure love is always unselfish; it pulls one out of their own convenience in an effort to make their partner or spouse happy. Robert concurs with this when he says:

> *"Love is that condition in which the happiness of another person is essential to your own."*
>
> Robert A. Heinlein[72]

True and pure love makes you selfless. Truth is that you get to think about your partner or spouse more than you think about yourself — you prefer not to eat in order for your partner or spouse to eat. You could sell or do anything to ensure that your partner or spouse is happy. Lastly, you will always seek for your partner or spouse's opinion before taking a decision to execute your plan; you will take their opinion into consideration to the amount of ensuring that you do not jeopardise their happiness.

Tolerance

---

[72]R. A. Heinlein, "happiness of Another Person is Essential to Your Own" [Online]. Available: https://www.goodreads.com/quotes/4964-love-is-that-condition-in-which-the-happiness-of-another [2021, November].

Tolerance is the ability to endure pain or hardship; it is the major ingredient for selflessness. In this segment, I will describe 'tolerance' as the ability to endure the pain and hardship that are involved in being selfless, that is, making your partner or spouse happy even though it costs your own happiness. Similarly, tolerance is about accepting your partner or spouse's flaws — taking them for whom they are. This is in accordance with Byron's opinion when he says:

> *"Tolerance is the mindful capacity to love, respect, accept the differences that make people unique."*
> <u>Byron R. Pulsifer</u>[73]

The truth is that no relationship will stand the test of time if the involved partners or spouses do not tolerate each other. Hannah did not gainsay this by affirming that:

> *"Tolerance and celebration of individual differences is the fire that fuels lasting love."*
> <u>Tom Hannah</u>[74]

Similarly, Jodi concurs that:

---

[73] B. R. Pulsifer, "Top 15 Tolerance Quotes In 2020 You Should Know" [Online]. Available: <u>https://www.epicquotes.com/top-15-tolerance-quotes-in-2020-you-should-know/</u> [2022, February].

[74] T. Hannah, "Tolerance and Celebration of Individual differences" [Online]. Available: https://www.passiton.com/inspirational-quotes/4405-tolerance-and-celebration-of-individual#:~:text=%E2%80%9CTolerance%20and%20celebration%20of%20individual,%E2%80%94Tom%20Hannah%20%7C%20PassItOn.com

"You don't love someone because they're perfect, you love in spite of the fact that they're not."

Jodi Picoult[75]

Lastly, Robert agrees to our opinions when he says:

"We love the things we love for what they are."

Robert Frost[76]

Certainly, you and your partner or spouse will get on each other's nerves sometimes — this is when your imperfections come to play — additionally, traits conflict (possessing opposite traits) may also be a factor however, instead of either or both of you to always make issues out of your imperfect actions, true and pure love should have both of you tolerate, improve and make each other better.

Care
Care is an act of showing empathy for your partner or spouse; it is the necessity to be concerned about their feelings, interests and well-being. This also has to do with selflessness so having discussed 'unselfishness' earlier in this chapter, I will not be saying much on this act. To care for your partner or spouse means to be very much concerned about their feelings, to ensure that their feelings are not hurt

[75] J. Picoult, "Love People's Imperfection" [Online]. Available: https://www.goodreads.com/quotes/13374-you-don-t-love-someone-because-they-re-perfect-you-love-them [2021, November].

[76] R. Frost, "Love Things For What They Are" [Online]. Available: https://www.goodreads.com/quotes/3710-we-love-the-things-we-love-for-what-they-are [2021, November].

and to make certain that their needs are met. This involves checking up on them, supporting them, providing for them, protecting them, improving them, including other good acts that favour a long-lasting relationship. In accordance with this, Felix says:

> *"Love is the expansion of two natures in such fashion that each includes the other, each is enriched by the other."*
>
> Felix Adler[77]

Similarly, Ovid says:

> *"Love is a thing that is full of cares and fears."*
>
> Ovid[78]

And lastly, Antoine says:

> *"Love does not consist of gazing at each other, but in looking together in the same direction."*
>
> Antoine de Saint-Exupery[79]

---

[77] F. Adler, "Love is the Expansion of Two Natures" [Online]. Available: https://www.brainyquote.com/quotes/felix_adler_387637 [2021, November].

[78] Ovid, "Love is Full of Cares and Fears" [Online]. Available: https://www.brainyquote.com/quotes/ovid_400208 [2021, November].

[79] A. D. Saint-Exupery, "Love Consists of Looking Together in the Same Direction" [Online]. Available: https://www.goodreads.com/quotes/2102-love-does-not-consist-of-gazing-at-each-other-but [2021, November].

In conclusion, I hope that I have been able to explicitly discuss some of the various characteristics of the truest and purest forms of love, that is, the true nature of love; unconditional, undiluted and un-deceitful. It is said that, "Love can never be perfect." Oh well, perhaps it means that what two lovers feel for each other cannot be perfect, but 'love' always remain perfect — in its truest and purest forms. "You may not be able to have a perfect relationship, but you sure can have the best of your relationship." That is, you can work towards perfecting your relationship and make it worth its weight in gold. If any of the discussed characteristics is missing in your relationship or you and your partner / spouse have been settling for a mediocre feeling that both of you call true love, I hope that this chapter would guide you in the interest of getting your relationship back on the right track, which will in return help your relationship to last long. I guess the question on your mind after reading this chapter may be: how can one then truly and purely love their partner or spouse? Edgar briefly advises that:

"We loved with a love that was more than love."
Edgar Allan Poe[80]

In addition to Edgar's advice, all that have been discussed in this chapter should guide you and your partner or spouse through how you can truly and purely love each other and also ensure that both of you feel the same way about each other.

---

[80] E. A. Poe, "Love More Than Love" [Online]. Available: https://www.goodreads.com/quotes/28979-we-loved-with-a-love-that-was-more-than-love [2021, November].

Chapter Ten

Basic Qualities of a true relationship

The qualities of a true relationship simply signify the level of excellence of a relationship, in other words, they denote the attributes of a true relationship — what makes a relationship true and successful. Having discussed 'A True Relationship' in Chapter Two, this chapter will only further expound it; it shall identify virtually all the qualities of a true relationship some of which shall be discussed while others shall be referenced to the chapters where they have been discussed in this book. The ones that shall be discussed shall also be supported with the beliefs and opinions of love experts, philosophers, scholars and other intelligent relationship contributors. This is to assist you to identify which of the qualities that are missing in your relationship additionally, to help you contrive them in your relationship. I will be discussing this chapter in a sequential manner; from a start of a relationship to where it should be with reference to a true relationship. Typically, what determines the future of a relationship is the beginning of such relationship: what brings about the relationship, the mindset and energy of the involved partners or spouses from the start and how both of them work towards achieving the best of their relationship. Before a relationship begins, it has been discussed in the Chapter Two that something must have led one partner to the other; this is what is referred to as Eros however, without regard to the desire and attraction, the qualities of the relationship have already started playing their roles.

Emphasising on John Donne's opinion which is quoted in Chapter Two, he says that *"love built on beauty, soon as beauty, dies,"* which suggests that if you make the beauty (not gender-based) of your partner a motive for your relationship then you may not have a long-lasting relationship. This is synonymous to Jodi's opinion which says: *"You don't love someone because they're perfect, you love in spite of the fact that they're not,"* and ditto to Robert's opinion: *"We love the things we love for what they are."* Although, beautiful things usually get much attention but true beauty is from within and only a true heart can see such beauty in their partner or spouse. Louisa M. Alcott also confirms that: *"Love itself is a great beautifier".* For the fulfilment of this chapter, the following qualities shall be discussed: Communication, Resilience, Apologetic-ness, Understanding, Supportiveness, Genuineness, amongst others.

Communication

After the attracting force (Eros), clearly one will like to get to know the person whom they are admiring better, and this is where communication becomes important. Paul says:

"The first duty of love is to listen."
Paul Tillich[81]

Similarly, to attest how imperative listening is, Brendan opines that:

---

[81] P. Tillich, "The First Duty of Love" [Online]. Available: https://www.goodreads.com/quotes/53994-the-first-duty-of-love-is-to-listen [2021, November].

"A man is already halfway in love with any woman who listens to him."
Brendan Francis[82]

Furthermore, a woman feels relieved and accepted when her man listens to her. Listening is part of communication, so before you even start to talk about yourself to that person you admire, you must try to listen (including nonverbally) to them perhaps: they are not in a good mood, running out of time, not in a conducive environment or other reasons that may thwart them from talking or expressing themselves freely. Other than these, even in the course of your relationship, you and your partner or spouse still need to listen to each other especially if one of you is going through a tough time and need to relieve their burdens. Furthermore, to eradicate all forms of assumptions, doubts and disputes in your relationship, you and your partner or spouse must learn to keep good communication with each other; this helps both of you to discuss potential issues in your relationship, most importantly, both of you must learn to listen to each other before taking certain actions due to annoyance. When it comes to falling in love, you may look out for some other qualities in your admired partner but when it comes to discovering the quality of love that your partner or spouse has for you, then you should start by finding out if they listen and how much they listen to you. The quality of communication between you and your partner or spouse in the beginning of your relationship (how often both of you talk about each other and what you really say about each other) and in the course of your relationship (how much you

---

[82] B. Francis, "Woman Who Listens to Her Man" [Online]. Available: https://www.goodreads.com/quotes/6523863-a-man-is-already-halfway-in-love-with-any-woman [2021, November].

share and confide in each other) determines the success of your relationship. Communication shall further be discussed in Chapter Eleven.

Resilience

Resilience in a romantic or marital relationship is the ability of a relationship to recover quickly from disputes, fights, grudges or malice. Without resilience in a relationship, it will be difficult for the involved partners or spouses to come back together or to love each other like they used to after an intense dissension which probably leads to domestic violence between them thus, it may impede their relationship from enduring for a long time. Resilience occurs in a relationship after a couple or spouses have been through a rough time but they still get back stronger in spite of their strife. Resilience is synonymous to flexibility. Like I stated in Chapter Four, I do have my principles and so do others; we may possess traits that makes us rigid and conservative but this does not work in relationships, especially marital relationship. While one may be rigid or conservative, their partner or spouse may be flexible or changeable, similarly, while one may be garrulous their partner or spouse may be a taciturn so the involved partners or spouses will have to strike a balance with a view to ensure that their traits, characters or principles do not affect their relationship. If you are in love with your partner or spouse, it indicates that both of you share your heart, mind, body and soul with each other, which makes it imperative that both of you make your principles flexible in order to fit in with each other, and not just your principles but your beliefs as well.

Resilience often comes after forgiveness and it does away with: disputes, fights, grudges, malice etcetera. Some persons may forgive their partners or spouses but still hold grudges against them, which makes the forgiveness half-done. If you and your spouse hold grudges against each other, you will not be loving each other like you ought to because love does not work with grudges and as a result, your relationship will not be experiencing resilience — your relationship will not bounce back from its tough times.

Understanding

Understanding is being aware of the meaning of something without having to misinterpret what is being done or said. Understanding your partner or spouse better will help you to predict and be aware of their action. When you understand your partner or spouse so well, you can tell when they are happy, sad, joking about their actions, serious in a discussion, and you can as well read the message in their silence, including their body language (nonverbal communication) as a result, you may never get to misunderstand their actions. Establishing how important understanding is in a relationship, Merge opines that:

> *"Life is the first gift, love is the second, and understanding, the third."*
> Marge Piercy[83]

In her opinion, understanding is next to love; it is the third after life and love. This explains the necessity of understanding is in all relationships. Every relationship depends exclusively on understanding; if you and your partner / spouse do not understand each other, even if one of you were doing something right, the other may mistake their actions for wrongdoings. As discussed in Chapter Eight, lack

---

[83] M. Pierc, "Understanding is the Third Gift" [Online]. Available: https://www.goodreads.com/quotes/407380-life-is-the-first-gift-love-is-the-second-and [2021, November].

of understanding is a sign of a faded love and similarly as discussed under 'resilience', misunderstanding is one of the acts that resilience do away with in order for our relationships to recover from their rough times. With all these being established, the importance of 'understanding' in a long-lasting relationship cannot be overemphasized, so you and your partner / spouse are advised to understand each other as much as you can if both of you really want your relationship to be pragmatic.

Apologetic-ness

Being apologetic implies when a person possesses the character of apology that is, to say sorry even when they have done nothing wrong. It has been discussed earlier in this chapter that 'understanding' is imperative in every relationship but you and your partner or spouse cannot get to understand each other overnight — it could take a few years before this is achieved — and in the process of getting to understand each other, you will get on each other's nerves a few times, and even more, and perhaps much more but if none of you possess an apology character, your relationship may end even before both of you learn to understand each other. Having to say sorry even when you have not done something wrong does not make you a fool, but it symbolises that both of you cherish each other so much that you do not want to lose each other and also want your relationship to last long. I will round off this segment with Judy's opinion below:

> *"Love means really having to say you're sorry."*
>
> Judy Gruen[84]

---

[84] J. Gruen, "Love Means Really Having to Say You're Sorry" [Online]. Available:

Supportiveness

A pragmatic relationship is potentially a lifetime relationship. This connotes that a pragmatic relationship has the prospect of becoming a long-standing relationship. Since you and your partner or spouse are meant to be together till the end of time, consequently, you become each other's responsibility — you have to support each other morally, socially, educationally, spiritually, emotionally, physically, mentally, vocationally, financially, medically and other spheres of life. Reiterating James Baldwin's quote which says: *"Love is a battle, love is a war; love is a growing up."* It is a necessity that you and your partner / spouse support each other to grow, that is, you must help each other to improve — make each other better. This is just-as-good as Felix Adler's opinion when he says: *"Love is the expansion of two natures in such fashion that each includes the other, each is enriched by the other."* You have not done enough regardless of how much love and care you have shown to your partner or spouse if you have not supported them in all spheres of life with respect to making them better, and factually, supporting your partner or spouse to be better even more than yourself shows your level of love for them. This is also supported by Robert Heinlein's belief which says: *"Love is that condition in which the happiness of another person is essential to your own."* It is always ideal for you and your partner or spouse to support each other. When this happens, it intensifies the flame of love in your relationship and as a result, makes your love wax stronger and relationship last longer.

---

https://www.chabad.org/theJewishWoman/article_cdo/aid/983681/jewish/Love-Means-Really-Having-to-Say-Youre-Sorry.htm [November, 2022].

Genuineness (absence of pretence)

Having discussed a pretentious partner in Chapter Six which is characterized by the intention of a person to impress their partner in order to have sexual intercourse with them, this act is contrary to 'Genuineness' — when a person is truthful, sincere and honest. Andre says:

> "It is better to be hated for what you are than to be loved for what you are not."
>
> Andre Gide[85]

Any act that does not conform to the characteristics of genuineness, such act must be one of the lust indicators that have been discussed in Chapter Six. In a view to making your marriage successful, you and your spouse must ensure that your words and actions are real, as only a genuine person can give genuine love and only genuine love can ensure a thriving marriage.

Other 'qualities of a true relationship' that have been and shall be discussed in this book includes: Tolerance (Read Chapter Nine), Trust (Read Chapter Three), Sacrifice (Read Chapter Four), Patience (Read Chapter Three and Eight), Forgiveness (Read Chapter Three), and Pragmatism (Read Chapter Three; Grow-up Together and Practised Love, and Twelve; Be More Practical).

---

[85] A. Gide, "It is Better To Be Hated For What You Are…," [Online]. Available: https://www.goodreads.com/quotes/14304-it-is-better-to-be-hated-for-what-you-are [January, 2022].

Chapter Eleven

Marital Relationship Determinants

Marriage is simply the union of two persons that creates a family tie and carries legal, social, and/or religious rights and responsibilities, to the exclusion of others meanwhile marriage determinants are simply what marriage depends on, that is, the factors that determines the longevity, sustainability, progression and successfulness of a marriage. This chapter shall be a reiteration and furtherance of related chapters. Let me ask a few questions that I believe you will like to get answers to: Why do some marriages experience certain challenges? Why do some marriages overcome certain challenges while others do not? Why do some marriages last long while others break down along the line? Why do some spouses endure in their marriages while others do not? The answers to all these questions depend on certain factors which shall be discussed in this chapter. The marital relationship determinant that shall be discussed in this chapter includes: The Nature of Love of the Marriage, The Previous Relationship Experiences of Both Spouses, Quality of the Marriage; Patience in Marriage, Tolerance & Endurance in Marriage, Communication in Marriage and Contentment in Marriage. All marriages depend on these factors and the successfulness of marriages depends on how these factors have been effectively managed.

The Nature of Love of the Marriage

Having discussed the Nature of Love copiously in Chapter One, you can easily relate the knowledge gained from it to what I have to discuss under this subheading. I shall be explaining how it can either be a hindering or facilitating factor in your marriage. Having discussed how the Physic-emotional, Non-physic-emotional and Spiritual Natures of Love and the 'types of love' in Chapters One and Two respectively, can be huge determinants in romantic relationship in the same measure, they can also be in marital relationship. I have stated in the previous chapter that marriage is meant to be a long-lasting union, but The Nature of Love into marriage determines the longevity of such marriage. This means that if you or your spouse have married each other merely for money, beauty, intelligence, speaking skills and/or others, then you may not be wrong to think that such marriage will not stand the test of time. Every other thing may fade away but real love will never fade! "Your mindset into marriage determines the successfulness of your marriage."

Although some cases may be different with respect to the reality of marriages; some persons may have negative mindsets into their marriages or fall in love with their potential spouses based on merely their physical features but in the long run, perhaps their spouses or circumstances give them a better reason to change their initial mindsets and they find something more reasonable in their spouses to fall in love with thus, they may get to have successful marriages. However, it is not reasonable to base our marriages on assumptions, mere physical features or ill-mindsets which make the success of our marriages dicey. For instance, if the type of love that is felt by a couple is meant to be merely Philia, and they both know that they possess opposite traits but due to one reason or the other, they decide to get married. Other than if the unusual happens, there is a high probability that they will have an ephemeral marriage because both of them may never understand each other and according to the Chapter Eight of this book, constant misunderstanding in a relationship indicates that the love has faded although the same chapter advises that the involved partners or spouses work on themselves, but in their own case, they probably have exhausted what instigated them into the marriage and there may be no reason to fight-on.

The Previous Relationship Experiences of Both Spouses

In Chapter Five, I have discussed how your previous relationship experiences may thwart you from loving your spouse utterly but in this chapter, I shall be discussing previous relationship experiences in an enhanced sense. In Africa, precisely Nigeria, most parents prevent their adolescents from engaging in romantic relationship. Their major reasons include but not limited to: they are too young for that, they will be distracted in their academics, they will develop an amoral attitude to sex, they will lose their virginities, however, they fail to see it from the positive side which are the experiences that they will acquire and as a result, help them to manage some issues that may surface in their marital relationship effectively. The adolescent and youth stages are when most mistakes and errors are exhibited in romantic relationship while marital relationship is the stage when those mistakes and errors are rectified, that is, they are put to rights — they are either avoided or managed appropriately. If one does not get involved in a romantic relationship in their adolescent and youthful stages before their marital relationship, it indicates that they will still be naive of the practicality of a romantic relationship, which may be a real big issue in managing their marital relationship.

Additionally, if they have not practically learnt the deceptive acts by deceitful partners as discussed in Chapter Six, then they are most likely going to experience a few marriage disappointments because they are most probably going to be victimized by deceitful lovers. For instance, if a young lover falls into the hands of a deceitful partner in a romantic relationship and experiences all the lust indicators that are exhibited by the fickle lover. As expected, the relationship did not last long and they have to move on. Having experienced the lust indicators, they may be of great help to them and avoid them being victimised by a fickle lover in their subsequent relationship perhaps marital. Our relationship experiences as adolescents and youths prevent us from repeating our mistakes, errors and negative occurrences in our marital relationships and thus, help us learn how to handle and improve our marital relationships. Similarly, our previous relationship experiences may contribute to us being doubtful, distrustful and cynical of our spouses which may as a result hold us back from making our marital relationships worth their weight in gold. In the end, our previous relationship experiences are imperative with respect to the mindsets that we may develop for our marital relationships and they may make or mar our marriages.

Qualities of the Marriage

Having discussed the Basic Qualities of a True Relationship in Chapter Ten, it is essential to go into how those qualities may determine the outcome of a marital relationship. Marriage has different factors that it depends on and this is based on how the involved spouses understand it. For instance, if a couple understands marriage to be a lifetime thing, then the basic qualities of such marriage will be tolerance, patience, understanding etcetera, which is what this book stands to achieve. Conversely, if a couple sees marriage from a different perspective as merely making love, having children, confiding in each other and providing for their family, then they may not fancy qualities like tolerance, patience and understanding. However, as stated earlier, this book is written to encourage spouses to have long-lasting marriages. So in this portion, I shall disclose the qualities that induce a long-lasting and happy marriage. The basic qualities of a long-lasting and happy marriage includes but not limited to: Tolerance and Endurance, Patience, Understanding, Communication and Contentment. These are briefly discussed below.

Tolerance and Endurance in Marriage
Tolerance is no doubt an imperative factor in a long-lasting marriage. Mignon opines that:

> *"No one has ever loved anyone the way everyone wants to be loved."*
> Mignon McLaughlin[86]

This signifies the imperfection of every marriage and the degree of expectation of the involved spouses. Truth is, no marriage will survive if the involved spouses lack tolerance and endurance for each other because none of them is perfect and just like Mignon says, 'both of them cannot love each other as perfect as they want to be loved', so they only have to appreciate as much love as they can give, tolerate and endure each other. Tolerance has been defined in Chapter Nine as the ability to endure pains and hardship, so clearly when you are being tolerant you are also enduring. Marriage

---

[86] M. McLaughlin, "No one has ever loved anyone the way everyone wants to be loved."[Online]. Available: https://www.goodreads.com/quotes/754063-no-one-has-ever-loved-anyone-the-way-everyone-wants [2021, November].

depends solely on how much the involved spouses can tolerate and endure each other. There may be a short limit to which you could tolerate your partner in a romantic relationship, but when it comes to a marital relationship tolerance becomes immense, this is so because a whole lot more things are involved. You may or may not be surprised to know that your spouse will feel free to reveal their true nature in marriage unalike in a romantic relationship, which denotes that you have to endure much more than you used to endure them in the course of your courtship. In spite of ensuring that your spouse possesses similar traits and characters to yours, you sure should know that they have their flaws just like you too which makes both of you imperfect. This is why both of you need to tolerate and endure each other even as you help each other to improve.

Patience in Marriage

Patience and impatience have been discussed in different chapters of this book, but Patience shall be discussed differently in this chapter. Since Patience has been defined as *"the act of waiting without losing one's temper or without getting angry"*, in equal measure, Patience in Marriage is the ability of the involved spouses to possess the act of waiting for a long time without losing their temper. Patience involves a persistent act of waiting in spite of the expected or desired result not forthcoming. To have a successful marriage, you and your spouse need to practicalize a lot of Patience. Patience is always involved in tolerance; this implies that in order to tolerate your spouse, you need Patience. Since marriage has been asseverated to be an agreement in which you and your spouse enjoy and endure each other, Patience is completely required during the process of endurance, so in order to have a successful marriage, you and your spouse must be patiently endurant.

Communication in Marriage

Communication has been affirmed to be an essential component in a successful romantic relationship, and this is no difference from a marital relationship. Speaking and listening to your spouse are two of the forms of communication and it cannot be gainsaid that marriage is built with words, even though it is imperative that you and your spouse complement each other's words with actions. Every thriving marriage is built on good communication and it depends on the communication built. A successful marriage depends strictly on how you and your spouse console each other, talk issues out with each other, inspire and brush each other up, tell each other how good looking you are, constantly remind each other of how much you love yourselves, and most importantly, listen to each other when either or both of you discuss your worries or burdens. Communication is very important in marriage in pursuance of keeping it afresh, saving it from marriage issues, saving the love from fading off and helping it to stand the test of time. If you really want your marriage to be worth its weight in gold, what do you do?

Contentment in Marriage

Contentment is an attribute of being happy and satisfied with your situation or condition, similarly, contentment in marriage is the act of being happy and satisfied with your spouse and the things that they make available for you. A successful marriage depends on the contentment of the involved spouses. When a marriage lacks contentment, either or both spouses may have to deal with issues like: constant contentions, dishonesty, extramarital affairs, pride, disrespectfulness and others, due to covetousness. Virtually all these acts have been pinpointed in Chapter Eight as the factors that indicate that the love in one's relationship is fading off. Lack of contentment, no doubt, will lead to either or both spouses cheating on each other which may in return impede the longevity or successfulness of their marriage. In the course of this act, the cheating spouse will exhibit acts like dishonesty, pride, disrespectfulness and others. Ultimately, to ensure a successful marriage, you and your spouse must be contented with each other and what both of you have got.

In conclusion, marriage has been discussed in this chapter to be a union that depends on certain factors referred to as indispensable. So, in order to have a successful marriage, you must ascertain that the nature of love of your marriage is genuine, learn from the mistakes of your previous relationship(s), ensure that the basic qualities of a successful marriage is not missing in your marriage, learn to endure and tolerate your spouse, avoid losing your patience easily, keep good communication with your spouse, be contented with them and what they can afford for you. It is also worth noting that all the qualities that have been discussed in some of the previous chapters only get essential in marriage. The next chapter shall elucidate the attributes of a successful marriage and what contributes to a successful marriage. Enjoy reading!

Chapter Twelve

A Successful Marriage

Conjecturally, virtually everyone who engages in marriage wants to be successful in their marriage however, it is a hard nut to crack. Although, while some will really like to be successful in their marriages, some may not even care, and perhaps most of those who desires to have successful marriages may not be willing to make the necessary sacrifices. As stated in the previous chapter, marriage is meant to be for a lifetime which is why you and your prospective spouse will be asked to take the marriage vows — *"...till death do us part"* — on your wedding day, but it is quite unfortunate that most people who take the marriage vows are either not aware of the hard work and sacrifices involved in keeping the vows or are never ready for marriage. Obviously, marriage is not an easy task and I must admit that marriage is practical on this account, circumstances in various marriages differ however, wisdom is needed in all marriages and it is what I will be sharing with you in this chapter. I am going to share my wisdom on how you can make your marriage flourish and also use the viewpoints or opinions of different love experts, philosophers and scholars to back up my points.

If you wish to have a successful marriage, I advise that you practice all and not limited to: Marry Someone Who Loves You More Than You Love Them, Develop We-are-in-this-together Mindset, Love Your Spouse Every Day, See All Changes in Your Spouse Positively Even Though They

Are Not and Help Them Improve, Be More Practical, Do Not Get Tired of Forgiving, amongst others.

Marry Someone Who Loves You More Than You Love Them

To have a successful marriage like I have stated in Chapter One, I always advise people to "marry someone who loves them more than they love the person." Although, the scenario of Lovers and Beloved has been examined in Chapter One but I will like to expatiate on how it may negatively influence your marriage. The reason for this advice is simply because it leaves you with the choice of making your marriage the way you want it to be. You may not be able to change others to love you but you sure can adjust to love others, in a more comprehensible statement — it leaves the choice of improving your marriage in your hands rather than in your spouse's hands. When your spouse loves you so much, you may start to think of doing away with your inappropriate acts and adjusting to your spouse unlike when you love your spouse more which leaves the success of your marriage in their hands. This is a choice between 'self-change' and 'changing others'. Putting the question to you, which is more ideal? Two of the benefits of marrying a person who loves you more are: it puts you in control of your marriage and, it helps you to manage your marriage.

Nevertheless, if you are in control of your marriage which suggests that your spouse would be the one loving you more, you should never make them feel inferior or regret their choices but rather, you should use that opportunity to make your marriage successful. This is because your reason for marrying someone that loves you more is mainly to have a successful marriage and not to make your spouse to feel inferior. I have heard and seen some spouses who take advantage of their other halves only because they love them so much and consequent upon that, they get maltreated instead of happy homes. This should not be the case with you because you now have the wisdom and responsibility of making your marital relationship worth its weight in gold. However, to avoid a lopsided affection, it is always ideal to strike a balance in your relationship as advised in Chapter One that: "Before you give the second (robust affection), you must ensure that your spouse has returned the first (middling affection)."

In conclusion, having explained the benefits of marrying a person who loves you more, it is not illogical to assume that you may also fall down such rabbit hole, so my sincere advise to you when this happens is the one I have given above, "always strike a balance; ensure that your spouse has returned the first level of affection before giving the second" — this is a very good principle of avoiding unrequited love.

Develop a We-are-in-this-together Mindset

I think that it is ideal that I begin this portion with Cate's viewpoint on marriage:

> *"Marriage is a risk; I think it's a great and glorious risk, as long as you embark on the adventure in the same spirit."*
>
> Cate Blanchett[87]

True love makes two souls to become one and as a result, the love shared between the two souls must be mutual and tantamount. True love is meant to be requited not held back.

[87] C. Blanchett, "Marriage is a Risk" [Online]. Available: https://www.brainyquote.com/quotes/cate_blanchett_453046 [January, 2022].

True love should never be lopsided. True marital relationship requires two involved spouses fighting together to make their marriage survive all the troubles thereof. Reiterating James Baldwin's beautiful contribution to love which says: *"Love does not begin and end the way we seem to think it does. Love is a battle, love is a war; love is a growing up"*, proves that true love should not be self-centred. The involved spouses must see each other's problems or troubles as theirs. A lady shared one of the experiences in her marriage with me and I will like to share in order for you to learn. The lady, as expected, thought that she could confide in her husband and one day when she returned from work, she tried to discuss one of her problems with him but she was so disheartened when he responded saying: "Those are your problems, not mine. Your problems are not my problems." This was the response that faded the love in her marriage. Although, they still live together but since then, the lady does not see herself being in the marriage anymore — her love for her husband started diminishing until she feels nothing for him no more.

If your mind is made of the ill-thought-out that your spouse's problems are not yours: it will not encourage your spouse to confide in you, it will make them feel alone in the marriage, it will make them think that perhaps you have started seeing someone else, it will put so much burdens and pressure on them and etcetera, in the end, what all these do to them is that it will make them sad and burn them out. On a contrary, if your mind is made of the principle that your spouse's problems are equally yours and that you can never be happy if they are not happy then your marriage would always wax stronger and stronger, because both of you will keep fighting the battle and war (challenges) in your marriage and grow together as Baldwin opines. That is what makes marriage a union; the marriage vows bind two souls together and make them one so, "There is never a problem for one soul in a marriage but rather, two souls as one fighting many problems."

Love Your Spouse Every Day

There are 24 hours in a day but just a second is enough to set one and their spouse apart. Sometimes, we have bad moods and this may affect our days and the people around us, including the very special people in our lives, but regardless of our bad days at work, home, road, visit, or anywhere, we must ensure that we do not allow such situation to thwart us from showing our spouses how much we love them. Barbara advises that:

> *"Love is a choice you make from moment to moment."*
> Barbara De Angelis[88]

This advises spouses to love each other every day in spite of their wrongdoings or bad moods. Like I always advice, 'do not go to bed angry at your spouse'. Loving your spouse everyday does not insinuate loving them in the morning and noon but going to bed angry with an unresolved issue but rather, it implies that you must express all the 'qualities of love' to them every hour, minute and second of each day, additionally, both of you must always remind each other of how much you love yourselves and how good-looking you are. Ultimately, buy each other nice things that make you smile, give each other your attention, discuss about your careers and goals, and motivate each other every day. These

---

[88] B. D. Angelis, "Love is a Choice You Make From Moment to Moment" [Online]. Available: https://www.goodreads.com/quotes/148504-love-is-a-choice-you-make-from-moment-to-moment [2021, November].

go a long way as it will not amaze or thrill either of you when your colleagues or flirts do any of them to you.

See All Changes in Your Spouse Positively Even Though They Are Not and Help Them Improve

It is said that, 'change is constant' and of course it is the only constant thing in life. As the world evolves and humans adapt to the evolving world, it changes us physically, mentally, socially, financially, emotionally, spiritually and vocationally. But the changes that individual undergo differs, as such, some changes may affect an individual more than the other or it may be more intense to cope with an individual than the other. What I am trying to say in a nutshell is that, for instance, if your spouse has a fascinating body-type when both of you started dating but owing to change, they loses their attractive body-type. You may want to start to think that they are not the one for you anymore but this thought is absolutely non-rational. If you really want to have a successful marriage and perhaps you are faced with such happenstance, you must do away with such thought. Maugham's opinion about changes in human is no different from mine and below is what he advises:

> *"We are not the same person this year as last; nor are those we love. It is a happy chance if we, changing, continue to love a changed person."*
> W. Somerset Maugham[89]

---

[89] W. S. Maugham, "Continue to Love a Changed Person" [Online]. Available: https://www.goodreads.com/quotes/41748-we-are-not-the-same-persons-this-year-as-last [2021, November].

In addition to Maugham's advice, it is ideal that you help your spouse to improve on themselves instead of having extramarital affairs. According to my instance above, you may improve your spouse's body-type perhaps if they are too chubby by having them enrol for a fitness programme and also monitor their consistency at the fitness centre. You may as well encourage them by going to the centre with them and assist them to execute some difficult activities. Additionally, age is another factor that may bring about a broken marriage; some spouses may start being repulsive and breed apathy for their co-spouses when they realise that age has started playing its role on them and thus, their glittering skin has started wrinkling and their sexual urge or performance is diminishing. They may resort to having extramarital affairs with a younger person, but this is clearly not the best thing to do if you really want your marital relationship to be successful. If you find yourself in this situation, my advice remains that you help your spouse improve themselves. Jeanne also advises that:

> *"Age does not protect you from love, but love to some extent protects you from age."*
> Jeanne Moreau[90]

Be More Practical

In a marital relationship, telling each other how much you love yourselves daily is not enough to secure a successful marriage but acting on every word you say to each other. If both of you have promised to: care for each other, spend

[90] J. Moreau, "Love Protects From Age" [Online]. Available: https://www.goodreads.com/quotes/164511-age-does-not-protect-you-from-love-but-love-to [2021, November].

time with each other, love each other forever, amongst others then you must 'practically' do as both of you have promised. How can a man claim that he loves his wife if he cannot give her a hand in the kitchen, prepare dinner when he gets home before her, assist her when doing the laundry and other chores? Similarly, how can a woman also claim that she loves her husband if she cannot assist him financially when he goes broke? To have a successful marriage, you and your spouse must persistently act on your claims.

Do Not Get Tired of Forgiving

Having advised that you and your spouse must love each other every day in order for both of you to have a pragmatic marital relationship, it is imperative that I complement my advice with the fact that you must also constantly forgive each other every day in order for you to achieve that. This is so because within 365 days in a year or 366 days in a leap year, there is a high probability that both of you will wrong each other many times, and for once or more times either or both of you may exhibit acts that may seem unforgiveable. Now, this is only an assumption for one year but both of you should probably be expecting even more in the first few years of your marriage especially if you are newly married although, 'the longer your marriage the shorter the problems of your marriage', provided that both of you never stops learning from your mistakes. However, you must keep forgiving each other and never for a moment get tired of it. Instead of thinking of letting go, let forgiveness be your resolution. Rumi postulates that:

> *"Goodbyes are only for those who love with their eyes. Because for those who love with heart and soul there is no such thing as separation."*

Rumi[91]

Additionally, Ella advises that:

"Just don't give up trying to do what you really want to do. Where there's love and inspiration, I don't think you can go wrong."

Ella Fitzgerald[92]

You can never be wrong for forgiving your spouse over and over because you want to have a successful marriage. Lastly, Dalai advises that:

"Marriages, even the best ones – perhaps especially the best ones – are an ongoing process of spoken and unspoken forgiveness."

Dalai Lama[93]

In conclusion, this chapter has been able to examine the possible ways that you can achieve a successful marriage, but in spite of discussing these few ones, I need to make

[91] Rumi, "Goodbyes are only for those who love with their eyes" [Online]. Available: https://www.goodreads.com/quotes/662262-goodbyes-are-only-for-those-who-love-with-their-eyes [2021, November].

[92] E. Fitzgerald, "Where there's love and inspiration, I don't think you can go wrong."[Online]. Available: https://www.goodreads.com/quotes/410685-just-don-t-give-up-trying-to-do-what-you-really [2021, November].

[93] D. Lama, "Marriage is an Ongoing Process of Spoken and Unspoken Forgiveness" [Online]. Available: https://www.goodreads.com/quotes/8555347-marriages-even-the-best-ones-perhaps-especially-the-best-ones-are-an [2021, November].

clear that there are other ways in which you can make your home happy and have a successful marriage. Without doubts, women are key elements in every marriage, and most times, understanding them will help men's marriages a great deal. In a marriage, understanding a woman is to understand that she is not meant to be understood but predominantly to be loved. Oscar posits that:

> *"Women are meant to be loved, not to be understood."*
> <u>Oscar Wilde</u>[94]

Some men may spend forever trying to understand their women instead of loving them. Of course, I am not saying that it is unreasonable for a man to understand his wife, but I am saying that he should not make it a priority instead of him to love her. Lastly, to have a successful marriage, you and your spouse must always think of 'forever', both of you must constantly bear that at the back of your minds and on this note Euripides opines that:

> *"He is not a lover who does not love forever."*
> <u>Euripides</u>[95]

Absolutely not! Ultimately, I think spouses' intentions and <u>mindsets into marriage go</u> a long way. If you and your

[94] O. Wilde, "Women are Meant to be Loved" [Online]. Available: https://www.goodreads.com/quotes/9994-women-are-meant-to-be-loved-not-to-be-understood [2021, November].

[95] Euripides, "He is not a lover who does not love forever" [Online]. Available: https://www.goodreads.com/quotes/208600-he-is-not-a-lover-who-does-not-love-forever [2021, November].

spouse do not have the intentions and mindsets to remain in your marriage in spite of the issues and challenges that may crop up in the course of your marriage, then you may find it difficult to fight for your marriage — either or both of you may not be willing to risk and sacrifice for your marriage — hence, your marriage may not stand the test of time. Contrarily, a true marriage is meant to last forever; with or without flaws, through rough moments, and through ups and downs. I will close this chapter with the below quotes:

> *"That's why love stories don't have endings! They don't have endings because love doesn't end."*

Richard Bach[96]

Conclusively:

> *"Love is the emblem of eternity: it confounds all notion of time: effaces all memory of a beginning, all fear of an end."*

Madame De Stal[97]

---

[96]R. Bach, "That's Why Love Stories Don't Have Endings" [Online]. Available: https://www.goodreads.com/quotes/32284-that-s-why-love-stories-don-t-have-endings-they-don-t-have [January, 2022].

[97] M. D. Stal, "Love Is The Emblem of Eternity" [Online]. Available: https://www.goodreads.com/quotes/109971-love-is-the-emblem-of-eternity-it-confounds-all-notions#:~:text=%E2%80%9CLove%20is%20the%20emblem%20of%20eternity%3A%20it%20confounds%20all%20notion,all%20fear%20of%20an%20end.%E2%80%9D

Epilogue

I hope that we have read from this book and have been able to identify one or two things that we are not getting right in our relationships. We must have as well learnt that loving our partners or spouses can take different turns and can be done in different ways. We may choose to love our partners or spouses forever or not — this assertion of mine is in accordance with 'The Power of Choice'. In spite of all that have been discussed in this book, I need you to know that romantic and marital relationships are practical. This expresses that individuals have different experiences when they engage in these activities, and their experiences solely depend on individual differences — traits, attributes and characters. This is why every individual cannot have the same experience in their relationship, so this book is only to assist you to adjust in your romantic or marital relationship.

The twelve (12) chapters of this book spells-out LOVE: family, acquaintanceship, friendship, romantic, sexual and marital relationships, including; self-love, obsessive love, unconditional love and flirtatious love. The Chapter One untangles the major nature of love; Physic-emotional, Non-physic-emotional and Spiritual Natures of Love, which is the first and imperative thing that you and your partner / spouse need to work on provided that both of you will like to have a long-lasting relationship and/or a successful marriage. The Chapter One also clearly distinguishes between a Beloved and a Lover, and provides a genuine lover with the understanding of identifying a Beloved partner or spouse so

133

that they may try as much to work things out with each other in order to avoid such act from affecting their relationship.

The Chapter Two clarifies the various types of love, which will assist you to recognise the particular one that you and your partner / spouse feel for each other. It also examines how a true relationship ought to be and indicates the signs that reveal one's relationship is true or not. Lastly, it advises us on how we can make our relationships true and suggests a few things that we can do in order to achieve a true relationship. Having discussed how a true relationship ought to be like, the Chapter Three examines the existence of true love in a relationship — how you will easily observe that love is prevalently extensive in your relationship; the signs and characteristics of love — which will have you and your partner or spouse to discern that love truly exist in your relationship.

The Chapter Four investigates the major factors involved in loving our partners or spouses truly which are Risks and Sacrifices. It explores the importance of risks taking and sacrifices in our relationships and how far they can take our relationships. It also examines the implications of the absence of these two key elements in our relationships. Chapter Five explains why some of us may choose not to risk and/or sacrifice for our partners or spouses. Certain reasons that may be responsible for such actions have been identified and briefly discussed, however, we are advised not to shut our hearts on love or victimise our partners or spouses in our present or subsequent relationships. The Chapter Six expatiates whom a lustful partner or spouse is — their characteristics and how to identify them. It is alleged that, "People who are sensible of love are incapable of it," this is why Chapter Seven juxtaposes and explains the pros and cons of being an experienced lover. Although, being an experienced lover may saves one's heart from being broken or save them from being victimised by lustful partner or spouse.

Sometimes, people stress themselves over relationships that just will not work out due to a reason or the other which either of the partners or spouses may not be aware of nevertheless, they will keep trying and perhaps think that someone else is responsible for the misfortune in their relationships. This is why Chapter Eight is written to expose us to the signs that will alert us when our relationships are growing weak or losing their freshness. They will in return assist us to take necessary steps in order to get our relationships back on the right track. Having familiarised ourselves with the signs of faded love in relationships, Chapter Nine elucidates the characteristics of the truest and purest forms of love. This chapter helps us to work towards having successful relationships. Although, some of the characteristics that have been examined in Chapter Nine are closely related to the qualities of a true relationship that are expounded in Chapter Ten, however, a good number of other helpful qualities are elucidated in Chapter Ten.

Chapter Eleven supports the opinion that to have a successful marriage, we must know what marriage depends on. This is why Chapter Eleven explores some marriage determinants which should guide us into and through our marriages. Lastly, Chapter Twelve explicates some indispensable elements that should assist us to have successful marriages. This is imperative as some of us only go into marriages without having the slightest knowledge of how to make our marriages successful. Finally, if all that have been discussed in this book can be duly acted upon, I believe that there will be less trouble to deal with in our marriages. Having the knowledge of something will equip one to make that thing better and this is the same with having a good knowledge of relationships. I hope that all these chapters provide some answers to our relationship questions, and some solutions to our relationship issues. Many thanks for reading!

*NB: It is important to note that based on the scenarios and occurrences that have been cited in this book, appropriate responses and solutions have been suggested which may seem like a contradiction to other solutions or advice that are given in other sections or chapters. To that end, I advise that you apply each of the advice given in each section or chapter accordingly.

Bibliography

About Author

Israel Adeogo Abejoye is a young diligent and prolific author of 'How to Become a Sports Expert' and 'Dark Cave: Philia's One Bad Wish'. He is a logophile and bibliophile so he finds it fun reading and learning new words every day — he tries as much to keep himself abreast of new words on a daily basis and likes to put them into practise in order not to forget. He is a potential football coach but also have a dream to obtain the highest academic degree in his field. He is a young altruist who derives pleasure in helping others — financially, physically, morally, mentally, academically, socially, and in other spheres of life and he could go out of his way so as to make people happy. Since he derives so much pleasure in writing, you can always expect more books to read from him.

Made in the USA
Middletown, DE
22 August 2023

37192914R00094